W9-BPN-553

ELIA J.H.S.
215 SENTINEL ROAD
DOWNSVIEW, ONTARIO
M3J 1T7

BRIDGES 1

S.D. Robinson
Series Editor

BRIDGES 1

S. D. Robinson · S. D. Bailey · H. D. Cruchley · B. L. Wood

Prentice-Hall Canada Inc., Scarborough, Ontario

Canadian Cataloguing in Publication Data

Robinson, Sam, 1937-
 Bridges 1

For use in schools.
Includes index.
ISBN 0-13-081944-1

1. Communication — Juvenile literature. I. Title.

P91.2.R62 1985   001.51   C84-099666-7

Accompanying Material

Bridges 1, 2, 3, 4 student texts and Teacher's Guides

Prentice-Hall, Inc., Englewood Cliffs, New Jersey
Prentice-Hall International, Inc., London
Prentice-Hall of Australia, Pty., Ltd., Sydney
Prentice-Hall of India Pvt. Ltd., New Delhi
Prentice-Hall of Japan, Inc., Tokyo
Prentice-Hall of Southeast Asia (PTE) Ltd.,
 Singapore
Editora Prentice-Hall do Brasil Ltda., Rio de
 Janeiro
Prentice-Hall Hispanoamericana, S.A., Mexico

Credits

Project Editor: Iris Skeoch
Production Editor: Jane Springer
Coordinating Editor: Miriam London
Production: Monika Heike
Design: Michael van Elsen
Illustrators: Victoria Birta, Loris Lesynski,
 Wendy Morriss, Karen Patkau, Karen Reczuch
Composition: Compeer Typographic Services Ltd.

ISBN 0-13-081944-1

2 3 4 5   89 88 87 86

Printed and bound in Canada by T.H. Best Printing
 Company Limited

Policy Statement

Prentice-Hall Canada Inc., Educational Book
Division, and the authors of *Bridges* are
committed to the publication of instructional
materials that are as bias-free as possible. The
student text was evaluated for bias prior to
publication.

The authors and publisher also recognize the
importance of appropriate reading levels and
have therefore made every effort to ensure the
highest degree of readability in the student
text. The content has been selected, organized,
and written at a level suitable to the intended
audience. Standard readability tests have been
applied at several stages in the text's preparation to ensure an appropriate reading level.

Research indicates, however, that readability
is affected by much more than word or
sentence length; factors such as presentation,
format and design, none of which are
considered in the usual readability tests, also
greatly influence the ease with which students
read a book. These and many additional
features have been carefully prepared to ensure
maximum student comprehension.

TABLE OF CONTENTS

ACKNOWLEDGEMENTS

The *Bridges* Series grew over a period of four years. It is not the product of any one person or of a group of people. Rather, it is the result of the work of many people, each of whom has left a special mark on the series.

As a result, we the authors of *Bridges* have many people to thank for their help and encouragement and downright hard work. We sincerely acknowledge these contributions.

Several teachers field-tested early drafts of chapters for *Bridges 1* and *Bridges 2*, pointing out the good and clearly telling us what would and would not work in classrooms. Our appreciation, then, to these teachers: Laurie Ball, John Barton, Brendan Bitz, Gordon Bland, Shelley Bryan, Irene Danaher, Lillian Fowler, Del Fraser, Shirley Gange, Wilma Gautier, Ellen Hagan, Donna-lou Holbrow, Eileen Leverington, Irene Loewen, Linda March, Phil McAmmond, Michelle Meugot, Lale Merdsoy, Al Mitchell, Dave Mumford, Donna Noonan, Cheryl Olischefski, Diane Page, Irene Sawchuk, Christine Vernon, Gerri Walker, and Marion Widlake. We have an extra thank you for Betty Thorpe and Mark Silverstein who pilot-tested an earlier version of *Bridges 1*. And we acknowledge, too, the help of Julie Ashcroft, Sheila Brooks, Don Cassidy, Bill Chin, Dan Clarke, Micki Clemens, Joan Lawrence, Harry MacNeil, Bill Talbot, and especially Karen Holm and Neville Hosking, all of whom cleared the administrative way to make this classroom work possible. And a grateful thank you to Christtine Fondse, Saskatoon Public School Board, and William Ewart, Regina Public School Board, for their help in writing and revising material for *Bridges 1* and 2.

We also owe a special thank you to those at Prentice-Hall who guided this series from its first stumbling steps to this finished product. Joe Chin and Monika Heike are to be commended for their untiring efforts in coordinating art and manufacturing. To project editor Iris Skeoch, and production editors Mia London and Jane Springer—thank you for the care and attention, and even love, that you have given to *Bridges*. Your cooperation and helpfulness got us over many a rough spot, and your professionalism has made *Bridges* a better series.

To Dorothy Greenaway, who worked with *Bridges* from its first stages, thank you for being a first-rate editor. Without your cheerfulness, your optimism, and your drive, we would still be mired in the jungle of first drafts.

The authors,
S.R., S.B., D.C., B.W.

Credits

Every reasonable effort has been made to find copyright holders of the following material. The publishers would be pleased to have any errors or omissions brought to their attention.

Sources

p. 8 Vincent Wall, "Big Bart". Reprinted from *The Canadian Children's Annual* 1976, Potlatch Publications Ltd., Hamilton, Ontario

pp. 26–27 Pierre Berton, *The Secret World of Og*, McClelland and Stewart Ltd., Toronto

pp. 43–44 *National Geographic World*, June, 1982

p. 44 Mary Moon, *Ogopogo*, Douglas & McIntyre Inc.

p. 59 Ronald Melzack, *The Day Tuk Became a Hunter and Other Eskimo Stories*, McClelland and Stewart Ltd., Toronto

Johnny Burke, "Kelligrew's Soiree" from *The Old Time Songs and Poetry of Newfoundland*, Gerald S. Doyle Ltd.

p. 85 Marion Endicott, *Emily Carr: The Story of an Artist*, The Women's Educational Press

p. 129 Monica Hughes, *The Tomorrow City*, Hamish Hamilton Ltd.

p. 137 All quotations from the essay "Food in Our Environment" by permission of Kim Kelsch

p. 151 "Jogging Shoes", Consumers Association of Canada, Saskatoon Local 102

p. 153 Elizabeth Kaufman, "Grandfather's Special Magic" from *The Dancing Sun*, ed. Jan Andrews, Press Porcepic Ltd.

p. 169 Janet Lunn, *The Root Cellar*, Lester & Orpen Dennys. Also available in paperback from Penguin Canada.
back from Penguin Canada.

p. 177 "The Wind Has Wings" from *Ayorama*, Raymond de Coccola and Paul King, Oxford University Press, Canada

p. 192 G. Joan Morris, "A Tale of Much Rejoicing" from *The Dancing Sun*, ed. Jan Andrews, Press Porcepic Ltd.

p. 214 "Boy slips from tight squeeze", Saskatoon *Star-Phoenix*, September 3, 1983

p. 225 Meguido Zola, "Doctor, Doctor"

p. 228 A.M. Klein, "Orders" from *The Collected Poems of A.M. Klein*, McGraw-Hill Ryerson Ltd.

p. 230 Joe Rosenblatt, "Waiter! . . . There's an Alligator in My Coffee"

p. 232 E.J. Pratt, "The Shark." Reprinted by permission of University of Toronto Press.

p. 235 Lyn Cook, *Jady and the General*

p. 261 James Houston, *River Runners*, McClelland and Stewart Ltd., Toronto

p. 261 Mae Worth, "Little Britches Rodeo". Reprinted from the *Canadian Children's Annual* 1977, Potlatch Publications Ltd., Hamilton, Ontario

p. 269 Ethel Wilson, "On Nimpish Lake" from *Mrs. Golightly and Other Stories*. Reprinted by permission of Macmillan of Canada and the estate of Ethel Wilson.

p. 270 Monica Hughes, *Gold-fever Trail: A Klondike Adventure*, J.N. LeBel Enterprises Ltd.

p. 277 George Clutesi, "How the Human People Got the First Fire", *Son of Raven, Son of Deer*, Gray's Publishing Ltd.

p. 278 James Houston, *River Runners*, McClelland and Stewart Ltd., Toronto

p. 281 Maria Campbell, *Halfbreed*, McClelland and Stewart Ltd., Toronto

Photos

Cover Shirley Wiitasalo, Canadian b. 1949, *The Shortest Route*, 1978, Oil on Canvas, 167.6 × 228.9 cm. Courtesy of Carmen Lamanna Gallery and the Art Gallery of Ontario, Toronto. Purchased by the Art Gallery of Ontario with assistance from Wintario, 1978. Photo by James Chambers, Art Gallery of Ontario; p. 1 Courtesy Saskatoon *Star-Phoenix* (*SP*), June 18, 1983; p. 2 (c) 1978 Saturday Review Magazine Co. (*SR*). Reprinted by permission. Photo courtesy of Metropolitan Toronto Library Board (MTLB); p. 3 (c) 1979 *SR*. Photo MTLB; p. 4 (c) 1970 United Feature Syndicate, Inc. (UFS); p. 6 Adapted from *National Geographic World*, July 1978; p. 8 top—(c) Walt Disney Productions; middle—(c) 1958 UFS; bottom—(c) 1978 UFS; p. 24 *Ottawa* Pegi Nicol MacLeod, #14203, Canadian War Museum, National Museum of Man,

National Museums of Canada; p. 27 from *The Secret World of Og* by Pierre Berton. Illustrations by Patsy Berton. Used by permission of The Canadian Publishers, McClelland and Stewart Ltd., Toronto. Photo MTLB; p. 42 (c) 1977 *SR*. Photo MTLB; p. 46 *Au clair de la lune* Alfred Pellan, National Gallery of Canada (NGC), Ottawa; p. 57 Courtesy *SP*, June 11, 1983; p. 60 *A Meeting of School Trustees* Robert Harris, NGC; p. 71 *Winter Theme No. 7* Jack Shadbolt, NGC; p. 74 *A Vision of Animals* Kenojuak Asherak. Reproduced with the permission of the West Baffin Eskimo Co-operative; p. 85 *Scorned of Timber, Beloved of the Sky* Emily Carr. Collection the Vancouver Art Gallery. Photo by Jim Gorman; p. 88 (c) 1959 UFS; p. 94 Courtesy Museum of Modern Art (MMA), New York; p. 99 Both photographs courtesy MMA; p. 103 Courtesy American Foundation for the Blind, New York; p. 112 (c) 1984 Archie Comic Publications Inc.; p. 114 *Floraison* Alfred Pellan, NGC; p. 128 (c) 1977 *SR* Photo MTLB; p. 130 bottom — adapted from Shirley Rinas; p. 132 Courtesy Gurdawar Sihra; p. 146 Adapted from drawing by Jenni Prokop; p. 150 (c) 1977 *SR*. Photo MTLB; p. 156 (c) 1982 UFS; p. 167 *Ghost Ships* B.C. Binning, Canadian b. 1949, 91.4 × 43.2 cm, AGO, Gift from the Albert H. Robson Memorial Subscription Fund; p. 170 Used by permission Grollier Publishers;
p. 172 The Red Cross name and emblem are protected in Canada under the Trade Marks Act. Used with the permission of the Canadian Red Cross Society; Federal symbol (bar/leaf) courtesy Treasury Board of Canada, Secretariat; Participaction logo courtesy Participaction; Big Brothers logo courtesy Big Brothers of Canada; Air Canada logo courtesy Air Canada; Olympic Symbol courtesy International Olympic Committee; p. 174

Child's Play Bob Iveson and Tom Gallie. Courtesy Century Saskatoon and the artists; pp. 181–182 Photographs reprinted from Photo-Story Discovery Sets #1, 2, 3, 4 and 5 courtesy Eastman Kodak Company. Set #5 is no longer available from Kodak; p. 183 *Alberta Rhythm* A.Y. Jackson. Reproduced by permission of Dr. Naomi Jackson Groves; p. 184 Photographs by Richard Hemingway; p. 185 VIA logo courtesy VIA Rail; CN logo courtesy Canadian Railway; Greyhound logo courtesy The Greyhound Corporation; p. 186 Photographs reprinted from Photo-Story Discovery Set #5 courtesy Eastman Kodak Company. Set #5 is no longer available from Kodak; p. 190 *Lake Superior* Lawren Harris, Canadian 1885–1970, oil on canvas, 102 × 127.3 cm AGO. Charles S. Band collection and family of L.S. Harris; p. 193 top — (c) *SR*. Photo MTLB; middle— (c) *SR* bottom— (c) 1975 *SR*. Photo MTLB; p. 194 (c) 1984 Archie Comic Publications Inc; p. 196 From *Crime and Puzzlement* by Lawrence Treat. (c) 1935, 1941, 1962, 1981 by Lawrence Treat. Reprinted by permission of David R. Godine, Publisher; pp. 212–213 Photographs reprinted from Photo-Story Discovery Sets #1, 2, 3, 4 and 5 courtesy Eastman Kodak Company. Set #5 is no longer available from Kodak; p. 218 *Untitled* Jessie Oonark, b. 1909, mixed media, 211.5 × 144.8 cm, AGO; p. 234 *Northern Nights* Frank H. Johnston, NGC; p. 236 left — (c) 1974 *SR*. Photo MTLB; right— (c) *SR*. Photo MTLB; p. 238 *Whale Sound* Suzanne Mogensen. Courtesy Dreadnought Publishers; p. 250 T.E.H. Jones *The Aboriginal Rock Paintings of the Churchill River*. Courtesy Saskatchewan Museum of Natural History; p. 264 *Pine Island, Georgian Bay* Tom Thomson. NGC. Bequest of Dr. J.M. MacCallum, Toronto, 1944; p. 273 (c) 1977 UFS; p. 289 (c) 1959 UFS.

BRIDGES 1

BEGINNINGS

Welcome to *Bridges 1*. *Bridges 1* is a book about communication — about how we communicate with each other in many different ways. For this reason it is a book about writing, speaking, listening, and viewing. The goal of *Bridges 1* is to help you understand how communication works. With this understanding you will become more skillful in your own writing, speaking, listening, and viewing.

Study this picture for a minute or so and then follow the directions in the Activity that follows.

Saskatoon Star - Phoenix

Activity 1

1. Use these thought starters to help you look at this picture:
   a) Who are the children on this *bridge* and what are they doing there?
   b) What has happened to them?
   c) What will they do next?

2. In your notebook, write about this picture:
   a) Use the thought starters to help you with ideas, and use any other thoughts that come to you while you are writing.
   b) Write steadily for two minutes, without stopping. Don't worry too much about what you write. Keep your pencil working for the two minutes. If you can't think of anything to say, write the word *bridges* over and over until something pops into your mind.

3. Share some of your writings with the rest of the class. Read your work if you feel comfortable presenting it in class.

This textbook is a kind of bridge, too — a metaphorical bridge that will lead you further into the study of communication. It provides you with the communication skills needed to connect you with the real world of communication. The *Bridges* series will help lead you onward from what you know already to what you'd like to find out in order to become a more effective communicator.

Your task now is to think more about communication.

Activity 2

1. Put the message of this cartoon into words.

2. Which do you like better, yours or your fellow students' words, or the cartoon picture? Why?

3. Which does a better job of communicating with you, the students or the cartoon? Why?

Activity 3

1. What makes this cartoon funny, the words or the picture? Why?

2. Make up another caption that could fit this cartoon.

3. Describe another cartoon that could be used with the caption: "Now *that's* the perfect bunt!"

"*Now* that's *the perfect bunt!*"

Activity 4

Use the following thought starters to think about communication and the purpose of this textbook.

1. Write one or two sentences in your notebook to answer each of these questions:
   a) What does the word *communication* mean?
   b) What are the different communication skills?
   c) Which communication skill(s) do you use most often? Why?

2. During the past twenty-four hours, what skills of communication have you used? Where? Use a chart to present your answer.

3. Why is it important to study communication?

4. What do you want to learn from your work in this textbook? Why?

5. Share your answers to these questions in a class discussion.

Activity 5

1. Write a short paragraph to yourself to answer these questions:
   a) What is communication?
   b) What do I hope to learn by studying about communication in this textbook?

2. Reread your answer several times during the year to remind yourself of your purpose in studying this textbook.

Chapters and Links

The main parts of this book are its *chapters*, which discuss the skills and knowledge of communication. Some of them will help you with the skills of *writing*. Others consider the skills of *listening* and *speaking*.

Still other chapters provide information about *language* and how language works in society. A few chapters deal with the communication skill of *viewing*, exploring the area of *visual literacy*. They involve studying the images and pictures that are a part of modern media, such as television and film.

Each chapter is not just about one skill or one idea. Several skills are integrated, or put together, in each chapter. In a chapter about speaking, for example, you can expect to find activities that help you develop other communication skills, such as those of listening and writing.

The *links* are the sections inserted between chapters. They contain a variety of activities designed to help you grow in specific skills, especially speaking, listening, and viewing. Others are there just because they are fun to do.

Your teacher will use these link activities in many ways. Some will be done before you begin a chapter; others, when you have finished a chapter. Still others may be done while you are studying a chapter. And some link activities may not be dealt with at all because they do not suit your class.

© 1970 United Feature Syndicate Inc.

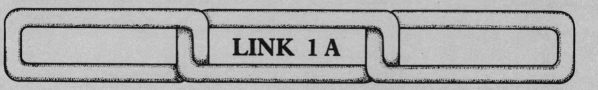

LINK 1 A

This activity is about getting to know one another. Here are the directions:

1. Your class will be asked to divide into small groups of about six students.

2. Each group will then divide into pairs. If you have an odd number of students in your group, set up one group with three students.

3. Each student *interviews* a partner to find out more about him or her. This activity works best if the students in the pairs do not know each other very well.
   a) Think of some questions you could ask your partner and write them in your notebook. Here are some examples:
      • Where did you go to school last year?
      • When you're not at school, what do you like to do most?
      • What is one interesting thing you did during your last summer holidays?
      • What kind of TV programs or movies do you like?
   b) Student A has two minutes to interview Student B and find out as much as possible about Student B.
   c) Then, Student B interviews Student A for two minutes.

4. Each pair goes back to the small group. Students in the small group introduce the partners they have interviewed to the other members of the small group. This introduction should be about one minute long.

Now six members of your class know each other just a little better!

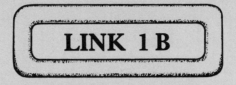

LINK 1 B

Here is another activity about introductions:

1. In your notebook, list ten words that come quickly to mind when you think about last summer.

2. Select the *one word* that means the most to you. Write this word on a separate page with large letters and sign your name to the page.

3. Taking turns, each member of the class will tell why his or her word is important. This talk should take about one minute.

4. Pin your word to a bulletin board to make a class display.

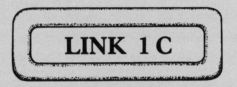

LINK 1 C

Perhaps you spent some time at the beach last summer. Here's a problem to see if you can still remember what it was like.

1. Look at this drawing. Which castle is completely different from all of the others?

2. As a whole class, discuss the way you went about solving this problem.

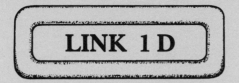

LINK 1 D

Perhaps you did some travelling last summer. Here's a quiz to see how familiar you are with *Canadian place names*. There are twenty-nine Canadian cities, towns, and villages hidden in this story. Many of them belong to big, well-known places; a few places are so small that only people who have lived in the area will have heard about them. Each province and territory in Canada is represented in the story.

1. Your class will divide into small groups, perhaps the same groups that you worked with to do Link 1A.

2. With each small group working as a team, look for the names in the story.
   a) Read the story quickly.
   b) Appoint someone to record your answers.
   c) As a group, go through the story line by line, telling the **recorder** what to write down. *Be sure not to underline in this book* — you don't want to make this task too easy for some student next year.

3. See which group is the first to find all twenty-nine names.

Big Bart and his girl friend, Victoria, were sitting on the terrace when Sydney rode up and told them that Wild Wally was back in the territory. Bart merely raised an eyebrow, then got up, said good-bye and hit the trail.

He rode to the lake, flicking a horsefly away from his golden palomino. He checked the south shore and the north bay. There was no sign of Wild Wally. Next he searched the hull of an old ship that was wrecked on shore, but there were no clues.

Suddenly an old Indian wearing a medicine hat rode up on a white horse. He told Bart that he had seen Wild Wally but that to find him, he would have to go north and cross many, many rivers. That is what Bart did and after the second river he came on to the grand prairie. There was mile after mile of choice land stretching out in front of him. Soon he met three farmers who were dividing up their wheat crop. "This is my ton," said one of them, "and this is Bill's and this one is

Edmond's ton." None of them had seen Wild Wally.

The third river was in flood. He crossed very carefully because of the swift current, but in spite of his best efforts, his horse stumbled and fell. He threw his rope to the other shore, missed, threw again and this time it caught around a big red rock. He pulled himself and his horse safely to shore, but he lost all his food. He had to exist on roots and leaves and many berries, which he cut with his yellow knife. Then one day he shot a big red deer. Now he could eat to his heart's content.

A few days later Big Bart came upon an old house. Behind it was a new castle. A man dressed in a brown cardigan was standing by the castle. When he saw Bart the man ran behind the castle wall.

"Who are you?" demanded Bart.

"Owen," came the answer.

"You don't sound like Owen," growled Big Bart.

"Oh, how does Owen sound?" quipped the voice.

"Now I know who you are by your voice," said Bart.

Wild Wally fled into the forest. Big Bart gave chase, but Wally had doubled back and he ambushed Big Bart. He kicked him when he was down and gave him an elbow in the stomach. But Bart did not give up. It was a long hard fight, but Big Bart finally subdued Wild Wally.

He tied him up and got ready to bring him back. But now he had to struggle with a wild windstorm. "Winds or not," thought Bart, "I'm going to bring him back to town." This he did and Wild Wally was put in jail. For the first time there was hope for law and order in the Territory.

Vincent Wall, *Canadian Children's Annual*

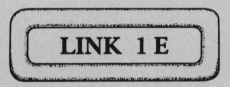

LINK 1 E

© Walt Disney Productions

The last activity asked you to work in small groups. This activity gives you more practice in solving a problem through **small group processes**.

Walt Disney drew two mice and called them Mickey and Minnie. These two characters have entertained children throughout the world for many years.

© United Feature Syndicate Inc.

Charles Schultz transformed his family dog into the cartoon character, Snoopy. Snoopy is loved by millions. His picture appears everywhere, not just in comic strips.

Jim Davis created a cartoon cat, whom he called Garfield. This fat cat is a real loafer, but he has many admirers.

A Group Problem

Now it's your turn to name a cartoon animal. These drawings show two animals, a dog and a cat. But they don't have names. Your problem is this: to find a suitable name for one of these cartoon animals. The name should be simple, but one that will appeal to a lot of people.

There is a special way of working together in groups to solve this kind of problem. This special type of problem solving is called **brainstorming.**

Here is how you do it.

An Experience with Brainstorming

Setting up. The class should divide into small groups. Four or five students in a group is a good number. This size allows everyone a chance to talk, and there are enough members in the group to give a large number of comments and ideas.

Step 1. In small groups, the first task is to select a **recorder**. This person will do all of the writing for the group.

Step 2. Define your problem clearly. In this case, the group has to decide whether to choose a name for the dog or the cat. Go ahead and make this decision. The recorder should write the decision at the top of a blank page: "cat" or "dog." If you want to share these ideas with your class later, you should use a large sheet of paper.

Step 3. Now comes the fun part! The small group should think of as many names as possible for the cartoon animal. Let your imagination run wild. Don't stop to discuss choices, and don't make any comments about them. Don't say the idea is good or bad. The task is to get as many ideas from your group as possible.

This process is called **brainstorming** for ideas.

The recorder's job is to write down all of the ideas that the group creates, without worrying too much about spelling.

Step 4. The recorder reads the ideas back to the group. The group selects a short list of five or six of the best names. This will require some discussion. But you should be able to agree upon some of the best names from your list.

Step 5. Your next step is to decide on the one best name for the cartoon animal. The group will have to discuss the merits of each name on the short list. After all of the reasons have been heard, the group decides upon the best name. You may have to take a vote to decide.

Step 6. The recorder reports the group decision to the class.

Afterward. After each group has reported its decision, the class might go through a **group agreement** round again (as in Step 5) to arrive at a class decision about the name of the cartoon dog and the cartoon cat.

Extension. Use the cartoon dog or cat to make a comic strip that shows something happening in your classroom.

STAGES IN THE WRITING PROCESS

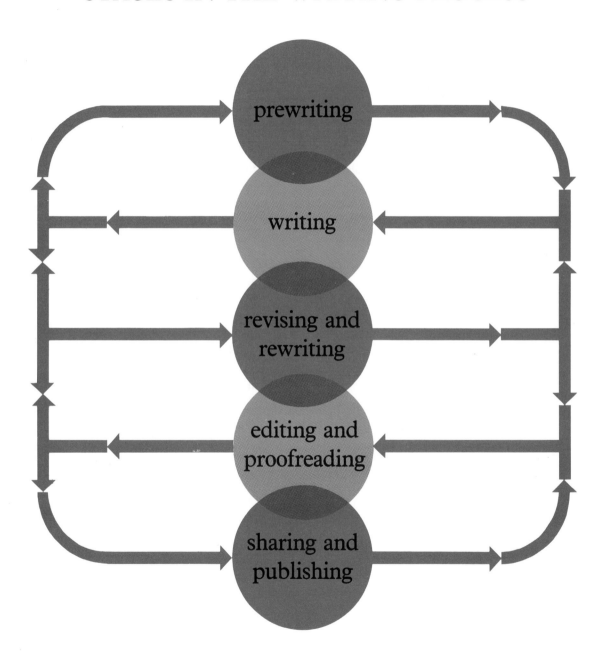

prewriting

writing

revising and rewriting

editing and proofreading

sharing and publishing

This diagram illustrates the stages in the writing process. It looks complicated, doesn't it? Have no fear. This chapter will explain it. You will learn all about each stage and how all of these stages are connected.

CHAPTER 1

EXPLORATIONS

GET SET FOR AN ADVENTURE

The Writing Process

Many people use their knowledge of the writing process to help them when they are trying to write something. This chapter will show you what these stages are and how they work to make writing easier.

But first, let's think about what writing is.

Exploring and Explorers

Throughout history, people have left their homes to seek out and explore new places. Some of these people have helped to build Canada. Their journeys and discoveries have contributed to our present way of life. Here are just a few of those travellers whose journeys into the unknown have helped build our country.

- *John Cabot* set out on a voyage of discovery in 1497. He landed on the North American Coast, possibly Newfoundland or Cape Breton Island. He discovered the rich fishing ground of the Grand Banks off Newfoundland.

- *Jeanne Mance* came to Ville-Marie, now Montreal, in 1642 with the first settlers. She founded the first hospital in the new colony.

- *Henry Kelsey* set out on an inland journey of exploration during 1690–1692 and became the first European to see the Canadian prairies. He also opened up routes for trade and travel along the Churchill and Saskatchewan Rivers.

- *Samuel Hearne* became the first European to reach the Arctic Ocean overland when he set out on a journey in 1771–1772. His northern travels took him along the Coppermine River and taught him to survive in the harsh northlands.

- *Thanadelthur*, a Chipeywan Indian woman, guided William Stuart of the Hudson Bay Company across the barrens to the Great Slave area in 1715. Known as the "ambassador of peace," she acted as a peace-maker between the Cree Indians and the more northern Chipeywan tribe.

- *Margaret McNaughton*, a member of a group called the Overlanders, set out from Quebec to journey to the gold fields of British Columbia. The Overlanders travelled by Red River carts, mules, packhorses, rafts, and canoe. Eventually they arrived in British Columbia, at Kamloops and Fort George. Their fantastic journey was unforgettable, but none of them struck it rich in the gold fields.

- *Martha Louise Black* set out toward another gold rush, the Klondike Gold Rush of 1898. She worked on her own claim there, managed a sawmill, and later was elected Member of Parliament to Ottawa.

- *Tagish Charlie*, with his brother Skookum Jim, discovered gold and started the Klondike Gold Rush. Skookum Jim was washing a dish-pan in Rabbit Creek and saw the gold lying in the water.

- *Maxine Brandis* is an example of a modern-day explorer. She and her husband immigrated to the northern lands on the Skeena River near Terrace, British Columbia, during the middle of this century. At the time when scientists were working to reach the moon, modern-day pioneers like Ms. Brandis were settling untamed sections of our country.

Activity 1A   Put Yourself on the Map

Each of the people described had an unforgettable adventure. Use the descriptions of their adventures to start thinking about an adventure that you would like to have.

1. Here are some ideas to get you started:
   a) If you could go along with one of the explorers, which one would you choose? Why? Write two or three sentences in your notebook to outline your reasons.
   b) If you were put in charge of a journey, would you choose any of the same destinations that these explorers did? Why or why not? Write two or three sentences about this question in your notebook.
   c) In your notebook, list two or three new frontiers or fantastic challenges that you face living in today's society.
   d) Choose one of these new frontiers or challenges and write a paragraph of several sentences about it in your notebook.

WRITING AND EXPLORING

Perhaps no two people would give the same reason if asked why they would choose to go somewhere. There are many different reasons why people travel, whether they are following a familiar road or taking off into the unknown.

In many ways, writing and travelling are alike. Here are some of them:

Travelling	Writing
• People travel in order to see new things and explore the unknown.	• Some kinds of writing allow you to imagine all sorts of fantastic new worlds.
• People travel for recreation and adventure.	• Sometimes writing allows people to enjoy adventures, real or imagined, in olden times or the future.
• People travel in order to revisit familiar places.	• People write about memories of sad or happy times in the past as a way of returning to familiar places.
• People travel to do business.	• Writing is a way to place orders, give information, ask questions, or make a request.
• People travel to make contact with other people.	• It is not always possible to talk face-to-face with others. Writing is a pleasant way to give invitations, say thank you, or pass along news.

Activity 1B   Your World of Writing

1. In your notebook, list three occasions during the past week when you had to do some writing. Beside each occasion, note the reason for writing.

2. In your notebook, list three occasions during the past week when you saw someone else writing. Beside each situation, give the reason why this person was writing. If possible, list people who are not in your classroom or your school.

3. Use your notes for a class discussion on this question: How important is writing in today's society?

Words written on a page allow you to communicate facts, ideas, or experiences to other people. You may be separated from them by geographical distances or differences in background, or the passage of time. Writing enables you to bridge these gaps between yourself and others.

Activity 1C   A Writing Record

The figure above shows how writing can connect people over a long period of time.

1. As a whole class, talk about the message it communicates to you.

2. On your own, think of two occasions in which you read something that someone wrote before you were born. Write them in your notebook.

3. Make a list of these writings as a class.

4. Is there any writing left in your school by students who have graduated? What kind of writing is it? Why did they leave it?

5. In your notebook, write a paragraph to say something to the student who might sit in your desk next year.

6. Read your paragraphs to a small group of classmates.

This last section has helped you consider what writing is. It's time now to begin to think about how you go about writing something. In other words, this next section will look at the writing process.

THE STAGES OF THE WRITING PROCESS

Here are the stages in the **writing process**. In the diagram, the stages have been set up as if they were steps. They seem to follow one another, from step one to step five, but when you write, things don't happen in quite this way. Writing is more complex than this diagram shows. The stages get mixed up. You might start with stage one and then move on to stage three, and back to stage one, and so on.

In this chapter, you will study the stages in the writing process one step at a time. This will make it easier for you to understand them.

And now—on to explore the writing process.

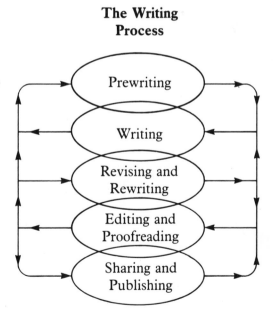

The Writing Process

15

Stage 1: Getting Ready—The Prewriting Stage

The first thing you must do when you begin to write is to think about your topic. You gather ideas in many ways: talking, listening, observing, reading, watching films, looking at pictures, and many other activities. Next, you may have to decide what **form** you need for your topic: a paragraph, a story, a poem, an essay. Often your assignment or writing task will make this decision for you. At other times, you will be on your own and you will have to make this decision. *The Forms of Writing* provides some examples of the different kinds of **writing forms** you might choose.

At this time, too, you consider the person who will be reading your work, and write so you can connect with this **audience**. Sometimes the person to whom you are writing is yourself.

The Forms of Writing

Activity 1D Exploring an Exploration — Prewriting

1. Think about an exploration you would like to be part of. For example, you might be part of a group that explores the floor of an ocean or the surface of a planet. Or, you might want to participate in a mountain-climbing trip in the Rocky Mountains. You could also think about an exploration that has happened, such as an adventure with an early Canadian explorer. Let your imagination run freely.

2. Work with a writing partner to answer the following questions. Go through all of the questions for Partner A first. Then go through all of them again for Partner B.

3. As you think about your own exploration, be certain to write notes in your notebook.

   Questions for Discussion Between Writing Partners
   a) What exploration would you like to be part of?
   b) Does this exploration occur in the past, the present, or the future?
   c) Where does it occur? What does this place look like?
   d) How many people are involved? Who are the main ones?
   e) What are some of the dangers involved in this exploration?
   f) What will be the value of this exploration?
   g) Does anything unusual happen? What?
   h) What is the best thing that happens on this journey? the worst thing?
   i) What is the biggest surprise to happen on this journey?
   j) How does this journey end?

Writing Partners

Explorers often had help. They worked and travelled with others who shared such duties as planning, packing, scouting, and keeping watch. When you write you may also work with one or more people. Sometimes you may work with only one other student: your writing partner. At other times, you may work with a group of two or more students: your writing team.   →

Here are some ways writing partners and writing teams can help each other:

1. *Prewriting stage*: Talking to your partner may help you get ideas, ask yourself questions, discover facts, and decide upon a topic.

2. *Writing stage*: You do most of the work at this stage, but your partner can help out if you're looking for the right word or you're confused about something.

3. *Revising and rewriting stage*: Your partner gets the chance to look over the first version of your writing and to offer advice. At this point, your partner may suggest how to improve your organization and ideas, by adding, removing, replacing, or rearranging words.

4. *Editing and proofreading stage*: A partner with a keen eye (and a good dictionary) may help you at this stage by pointing out such problems as spelling, capitalization, and punctuation problems.

5. *Sharing and publishing stage*: Now that you've completed the finished copy, your partner is your first official audience and can suggest who else would enjoy reading your work.

Activity 1E   Choosing a Form

Continue to work with a writing partner to answer these questions:

1. Which one of the writing forms can you write most easily?

2. Which of these forms seems most suitable for the topic you chose in Activity 1D?

3. What other form might you use for this same topic?

4. Is there another form which you could use for your topic that is not listed?

5. What form do you think is best to write a story about your exploration?

Stage 2: Beginning to Write — The Writing Stage

Now it's time to work alone. You have reached the writing stage — a time to explore your ideas through your writing. Perhaps you might use pencil at this stage so that you can more easily make changes in your writing later.

Activity 1F   Writing About Your Exploration

1. Reread the notes you made for Activity 1D.

2. Choose the set of notes that interests you most from your ideas about these things: the dangers, the unusual happening(s), the best happening(s), the worst happening(s), the biggest surprise.

3. Pick up your pencil and get your ideas down on your page as quickly as you can.
   Note: Write quickly. Concentrate on your ideas. Don't worry about such things as spelling and punctuation at this stage.

4. Repeat Steps 1 to 3 with another story from your exploration: dangers, good things, bad things, surprises.

You now have two paragraphs that tell about your adventure.

Stage 3: Finishing Your Story—Revising and Rewriting

After you have written the two stories for Activity 1F, you can work with a writing partner to make improvements in them. You must keep one thing in mind. Your writing partner, or your writing group, will give you lots of advice at this stage in the writing process. But it is advice only. You do not have to accept it. This is your story, your piece of writing, and you have the final decision about it.

Activity 1G Revising Your Story

1. **Work together to consider these revision activities:**
   a) **Exchange your stories with your writing partner.**
   b) **Partner A reads aloud both of the stories that he or she wrote for Activity 1D.**
   c) **Decide which of the two stories you like better. Discuss why you liked it better.**
   d) **Repeat steps b and c for Partner B's stories.**

2. **Work on your partner's story, following these directions:**
   a) **Partners A and B exchange the stories they selected as the better ones.**

b) Read your partner's story again, silently.

c) At the bottom of your partner's page, write two or three sentences explaining why you liked this story.

d) Write a new beginning sentence for your partner's story. (A beginning sentence for a paragraph is also called a topic sentence.)

e) Give your partner five words that he or she could use instead of the words already chosen.

> *Example:* It was a nice day. The boy walked down the street.
> *Suggestions:* *nice* day → *spring* day.
> the *boy* → Nathan
> the *street* → Robie Street

3. On your own, revise your story.

a) Reread your own story, after your writing partner has returned it to you.

b) Think about the advice your partner has given you. If you like it, use it in the next stage. If you don't like it, don't use it.

c) Read and think about your story once more. Add any changes you can think of.

4. Rewrite your story to make a good copy of it.

Stage 4: Solving Problems—Editing and Proofreading

In Stage 3 you were mainly concerned with the ideas in your story and with the words you used to express these ideas. In Stage 4, your task is to get your writing ready to share it with an audience beyond your writing partner. You may get help from several sources at this stage:

- Your writing partner or writing team may point out mistakes in spelling, punctuation, or sentence structure.
- A dictionary will give you correct spelling.
- A thesaurus will suggest colourful words to replace dull or inappropriate language.

Activity 1H   Last-Minute Touches

1. Exchange your work with your writing partner. Read your partner's work carefully.

2. Use this *copyediting checklist* to help your partner correct some common mistakes.

> *Copyediting Checklist*
> - Check for correct spelling.
>   Watch for these common mistakes with homophones:
>   to-too-two   hear-here
>   their-there-they're   it's-its
>
> - Check punctuation marks at the end of each sentence:
>   Do all questions have a question mark?
>
> - Check capital letters.
>   Does this writing use capital letters for the names of all cities, provinces, countries, and people's names?

3. After your partner gives your story back to you, look at the comments carefully.

4. Use the checklist to go through your story once again, to look for any of these common mistakes.

5. If you have only a few editorial corrections, make them on your copy. If there are a number of corrections, rewrite your story one more time. People will be more likely to read your story if it is well presented.

Stage 5: Arriving — Sharing and Publishing

The final stage in the writing process is sharing and publishing your finished work. You can do this in many ways.

Activity 1I From Me to You

1. Here are some suggestions for sharing your stories:
   a) You and your writing partner may read your stories aloud to members of another writing group.
   b) Your class may have a sharing session during which everyone exchanges writings with other students or reads them aloud to the class.
   c) Your class may publish a writing booklet or arrange a bulletin board display.
   d) You may invite a guest — such as your principal or librarian — to listen as your class reads some of your stories.

2. As a class, brainstorm to come up with other ideas for publishing and sharing your written work. Be as imaginative as you can. You may want to use tape recorders and videotapes and computers if they are available.

3. Then go ahead and share your work.

Learning to Map Out Your Thoughts

Exploring ideas when you write is much like exploring a new place. You may have many unusual and interesting experiences along the way. At the end, you may come up with something completely unexpected.

When you write, you are exploring your own mind, ideas, and opinions. What you put down on paper is a kind of map that shows other people the route your thoughts took. One way to make sure your map is easy to understand is to follow all the stages in the writing process. Other chapters in this book will show you more about the writing process.

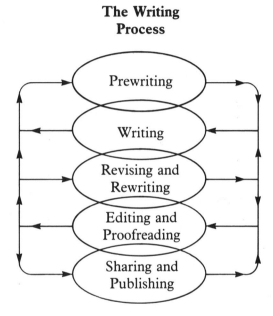

The Writing Process

- Prewriting
- Writing
- Revising and Rewriting
- Editing and Proofreading
- Sharing and Publishing

LINK 2 A

Chapter 1 took you on an imaginary journey. This activity will take you on a journey into Canada's past. This painting was done by Pegi Nicol MacLeod, a Canadian artist. It is titled *Ottawa, 1945*. The painting shows Confederation Square as seen from Elgin Street during World War II.

1. Look at the painting to note as many details as possible. List these details in your notebook.

Ottawa, 1945 Pegi Nichol MacLeod

2. Think about this painting. Use these **thought starters** to get going:
   a) How does the painting make you feel?
   b) What are the people in the painting doing? How are they feeling? Why?
   c) In which direction do most of the lines in this painting go? Why?
   d) What do you think about the soldier on the right side? Why is he larger than the other figures in the painting? What do you think of the soldier just to his left?

3. Construct a **thought web** in your notebook to record your reactions to *Ottawa, 1945*. These directions will help you with the thought web:
   a) Draw a small circle in the centre of your page. Write *Ottawa, 1945*, inside the circle.
   b) Add to this circle the thoughts and feeling you discovered as you did 2. Include any new ideas you have as you construct this thought web.
   Here is an example:

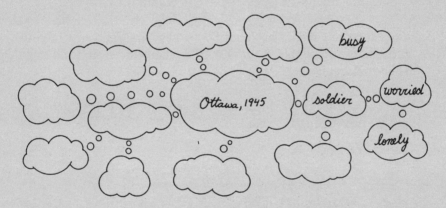

4. Have a second look at your thought web. Choose three sections, or connected circles, which interest you.

5. In your notebook, write a short paragraph of at least six sentences that gives your response to *Ottawa, 1945*.
   a) Use the three sections you chose in 4 as the beginning of your paragraph.
   b) Try to include as many details from the painting as possible in your paragraph. You will need these details for the next activity.

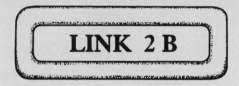

LINK 2 B

In this activity, you will use the paragraph you wrote in *Link 2A* to practise **listening**. You will have to concentrate to listen for details and to remember them.

1. A team of three students goes to the front of the classroom. Taking turns, each student reads his or her paragraph about *Ottawa, 1945*.

2. The other students in the class listen to these three readings, following these directions:
   a) Listeners are not allowed to take notes. Hide your pencil!
   b) Listeners should have *Ottawa, 1945*, open on their desks.
   c) Listeners try to remember each detail from the painting mentioned in any of the three paragraph readings.

3. When the third reader has read his or her paragraph, list in your notebook the details about *Ottawa, 1945* that were given in all three of the paragraphs.

4. Your class may repeat this activity several times, just to give you practice in listening for details.

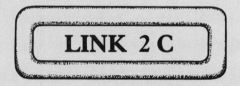

LINK 2 C

This link activity contains a **dictation passage**. Here is how dictation passages should be used. First, your teacher will read the passage to you, while you listen with your text closed. Next, he or she will reread the passage while you write in your notebook. As your teacher reads the passage a third time, check your work. Last, your teacher will tell you how to use this text to correct your dictation.

This dictation passage comes from Pierre Berton's *The Secret World of Og*. You may have already read this book. The passage reviews capital letters and periods at the end of sentences. Also, be certain to indent the first sentence to show that you are writing a paragraph.

Patsy, by this time, was trudging across the field in the bright afternoon sunlight, heading for the home of the Terrible Twins, who lived down the road. The twins were her closest friends and allies, being exactly the same age. Like Patsy they had angelic faces and blonde heads. Like Patsy, they liked frogs better than people and snakes better than frogs. The three of them had once captured a skunk and put him in a paper shopping bag and taken him home. They said they did this to surprise Mother, and of course, it had surprised her quite a bit.

Pierre Berton, *The Secret World of Og*

Patsy Berton

Question: What *one* word in this dictation passage tells you that the Terrible Twins are girls?

Extension: Does this passage bring back memories? Does it take you on a journey back to your own childhood? Exchange memories in class. How did you surprise your Mother? And how did you try to fool your Dad?

CHAPTER 2

JOURNEYS

LET YOUR WRITING DO THE WALKING

Journeys are always interesting. You can never be sure of exactly what you will see or do. A journey may provide unlimited chances to explore new places and enjoy new experiences.

Imagine how exciting it would be if you could plan your own journey! You would be able to choose where to go, how to travel, and what to do. If you could be your own travel agent, you could build your own adventure.

This chapter offers you a number of choices for adventure. You will be able to choose one of several possible journeys to write about. As you plan and write your journey, you will be following the **writing process** from start to finish.

Setting Up Your Writing Folder

During this year you will be doing a lot of writing: paragraphs, reports, short essays, poems, critical analyses.

You will need a place to store all of your work. Why not create a writing folder? This folder could be a binder, a plain file folder, or even a box.

Make a table of contents for your folder. Keep your work neatly in order. You will want to find things easily when you look for something you wrote earlier.

During the year, you may go back and reread some of the writing you have done. This is an excellent way to find out how you are growing in your writing skill.

Here are some guidelines for your folder:

1. Keep all of your finished work in your folder.

2. Make certain that your work is neat and that it is done as well as you can.

3. Use the same size paper for all assignments.

4. Reread your work from time to time to check on how you are doing.

5. Keep your table of contents up to date.

BUILDING YOUR OWN ADVENTURE

Now get set to travel! You are about to build your own adventure. You have a choice of four travelling companions to go with you on three different journeys. This picture shows you the four travellers together, waiting for your adventure to begin.

Each of the travellers can take you on a different kind of journey. Read on. You will find a description of the adventure each traveller can offer, as well as descriptions of the writing projects you will be asked to do about the adventure you choose. You will have a chance to talk and think about the three adventures before you make your choice.

Choice 1: The Cruise

You have just been appointed the cruise director of a luxury space-liner, the *Solar Princess*. Your first big job is to decide where the *Solar Princess* should go on its next cruise. The passengers expect to travel somewhere in Earth's solar system. They expect to see things that are *out of this world*.

1. If you choose this adventure, your writing project will be to write about the cruise the *Solar Princess* takes.

2. Your story will be included in a brochure for future passengers.

3. You should describe the three places the space-liner goes and what you and the passengers will see.

4. You may want to include illustrations.

Choice 2: The Quest

Two young people, a prince and a princess, live in castles separated by many dangers. These dangers are shown on the map of their two kingdoms. In the centre of the map is the *Enchanted Garden*, where the prince and princess can meet safely. In order to reach the garden, they must each confront several obstacles. Study the map carefully so you know what dangers threaten them.

1. If you choose this adventure, your writing project will be to write about the journey taken by either the prince or the princess.

2. Imagine that you are either the prince or the princess. Think of what your journey will be like. Write the story of your adventures from the time you leave your castle to the time when you arrive at the Enchanted Garden.

PRINCE CASTLE

PRINCESS CASTLE

HAUNTED HILLS

MARSH

FOREST OF TERROR

RAGING RIVER

QUICK-SAND

TROLLS

ENCHANTED GARDEN

Choice 3: The Weekend Wanderer

Imagine that you have a chance to win a luxury trip to any place you want to go. All you have to do is solve this puzzle and write a story about the solution.

The Puzzle: You must plan a weekend trip to some place at least two hundred kilometres away, using four different methods of travel: a horse, a snowmobile, a hot air balloon, and a ten-speed bike. You may use them in any order, and you may add anything else you wish. However, your trip can last only from Friday night to Sunday evening. You must reach your destination within two days.

1. If you choose this adventure, your writing project will be to write about the trip you planned and how you solved the puzzle.

2. Solving the puzzle means that you found ways to use the horse, snowmobile, hot-air balloon, and ten-speed bike to take you to your destination.

3. You should explain where you went and how you used these four things. The contest judges who read your story will want to see an interesting solution to the puzzle.

GETTING SET FOR ADVENTURE

Now you know what kind of adventures lie ahead. All you have to do is choose the one you will take. Before you choose, you may want to talk about some of the ideas you could use when you write about your adventure. This is an important part of the **prewriting stage**.

Activity 2A Choosing Your Adventure

In this activity you will work with a group of students to talk about the three adventures: *The Cruise, The Quest,* and *The Weekend Wanderer*. After you have talked about these adventures, you will choose one of them to write about.

1. As a group, talk about these questions. Each member of the group should give at least one answer or suggest one idea.

a) Which of the three journeys do you think would be the most exciting?

b) Why do you think so?

c) On each of the three journeys, what is the greatest challenge or danger that you could face?

d) Suggest one way in which the cruise director, the prince or princess, and the weekend wanderer might be alike.

2. As a class, share the ideas you have gathered in the small groups.

3. Use the ideas from group discussion and class discussion. Write out answers to each of the above questions.

4. Think carefully about what you discussed and wrote in your notebook.

a) Choose the adventure *you* want to take.

b) Find a *writing partner* who has chosen the same adventure as you to work with you as you complete your journey through the writing process in the rest of this chapter.

ON THE ROAD TO ADVENTURE

Now that you have made your choice, you are ready to begin to think about your adventure! Follow the directions and the arrow to help you write your story.

Prewriting Your Adventure

You already did some prewriting when you discussed your choice of adventure. Now that you have made your choice, more prewriting will help you build up your bank of writing ideas.

Work with your writing partner to talk about the adventure you chose. If you chose 'The Cruise' do Activity 2B. If you chose 'The Quest' do Activity 2C. If you chose 'The Weekend Wanderers' do Activity 2D.

Activity 2B   Prewriting: The Cruise

1. What would the job of a cruise director be like?

a) What kind of information would a cruise director need to know about the passengers?

b) Why would people want to take a space cruise?
c) What would they like to do that they cannot do back on Earth?

2. What ideas can you find in other sources and from other people?
   a) How could a *real* travel agent help you with your story?
   b) What could you learn at a planetarium?
   c) Who or what else could give you ideas or information about a space cruise?

3. What kind of information could you find in a library to help you write about a space cruise?
   a) What might you want to find out in the library about the Earth's solar system?
   b) Which planets are the most interesting? How could you find out?
   c) What do you need to find out about special equipment that human beings might need to visit other planets?
   d) How could you find out about other parts of the solar system that might be worth seeing?

Go on to  Activity 2E

Activity 2C Prewriting: The Quest

1. What does the map of the two kingdoms on page 32 tell you?
   a) What solutions can you think of for each of the dangers in the map?
   b) How do you think the prince or princess would feel about the journey?
   c) What is the greatest danger shown on the map?
   d) What kind of person would take a journey through such great danger?

2. Which is the best route for the prince to take?
   Which is the best route for the princess to take?
   a) Why do you choose these two routes over the others?
   b) What are the dangers that lurk along the way?
   c) What different problems will the prince and the princess have on their separate journeys?

3. How would the prince and princess prepare for this journey?

a) If you were the prince or princess, what would you think about as you prepared for this journey?
b) What would you take with you on the journey?
c) What equipment would you take to protect yourself?
d) What might you think about as the journey went on?
e) If you could take a companion, who would it be?

Go on to  Activity 2F

Activity 2D Prewriting: The Weekend Wanderer

1. What would such a trip be like?
   a) How far and how fast can you travel with each of the four — horse, snowmobile, hot-air balloon, ten-speed bike?
   b) What kind of conditions do you need to travel with each of them?
   c) Can you add or combine any of them with something different in order to change the way you travel?
   d) What is the greatest danger you could face with each of them?

2. What might happen while you are on the trip?
   a) What is the most interesting or unusual place you might try to reach?
   b) What dangers or problems could develop as you used each of the four means of travel: horse, snowmobile, hot-air balloon, ten-speed bike?
   c) What kind of exciting details could you add to impress the contest judges?
   d) In what ways could you use two of the four means of travel at any one time?

3. What information can you find at the library to help you plan this trip?
   a) What ideas can you get from maps? from reference books?
   b) What are some possible routes you might take?
   c) What can you find out about the climate along your route? the road conditions? places to eat and sleep?
   d) What other types of transportation could you use as well as the four you have been given?

Go on to Activity 2G

Writing the First Draft of Your Adventure

Now that you have done some talking and reading and thinking about your adventure, you should be ready to write a first draft. Use a pencil and some newsprint or some scrap paper. Write your ideas down quickly, without being too concerned about spelling and punctuation.

Activity 2E   Writing: The Cruise

What will happen on the cruise you have arranged for the *Solar Princess*? Use the ideas you have gathered to write the story of your adventures on board the space-liner. You may decide to tell the story of just one day — the most dangerous or the most exciting day.

Go on to Activity 2H

Activity 2F   Writing: The Quest

Imagine you are either the prince or the princess. Think about what your journey will be like. Now, write the story of your adventures, from the time you leave your castle to the time you arrive at the Enchanted Garden.

Go on to Activity 2I

Activity 2G   Writing: The Weekend Wanderer

Now you are ready to write the story of how you reached a place at least two hundred kilometres away, using four methods of travel: horse, snowmobile, hot-air balloon, ten-speed bike. Use the ideas

you have gathered to tell about your adventures along the way. You may decide to spend most of the time telling about the most dangerous, the most surprising, or the most exciting thing you did.

Go on to Activity 2J

Revising and Rewriting Your Adventure

Work with a writing partner to think some more about your adventure. Exchange papers and offer each other some ideas to help make your adventure more interesting. Write your advice on a separate page and give it to your partner. Remember: Your partner is giving you advice only. You can choose to accept or ignore this advice.

When you have used your partner's advice and thought about your adventure one more time on your own, write another draft of your story.

Activity 2H Revising: The Cruise

1. Exchange papers and answer the following questions about your writing partner's paper.
   a) Show your partner one place in his or her paper where you would have liked more information about an event that is taking place.
   b) Ask one question about the place the *Solar Princess* visits so that you will know more about the place.
   c) Suggest for your partner one event that would add more excitement or suspense to the adventures of the *Solar Princess*.
   d) Suggest for your partner a different order in which the events of the story might take place.

2. When you get your partner's comments, read them carefully. Keep these ideas in mind as you think some more about your own story:
   a) What advice from your partner is worthwhile? How can you use it to change your story?
   b) Is there any advice you disagree with?
   c) What changes can you now make to your story?

Go on to Activity 2K

Activity 2I   Revising: The Quest

1. Exchange papers and answer the following questions about your writing partner's paper.
   a) Ask about any place where something on the map is not clearly described in the story.
   b) Suggest a different solution to one of the dangers on the way.
   c) Ask one question about something the prince or princess did.
   d) Suggest a different order in which events might take place.

2. When you get your partner's comments, read them carefully. Keep these ideas in mind as you think about your story:
   a) Do any of your partner's suggestions give you new ideas about how to change and improve your story? How?
   b) Do you disagree with any of your partner's advice?
   c) What changes do you now want to make to your story?

Go on to Activity 2K

Activity 2J   Revising: The Weekend Wanderer

1. Exchange papers and answer the following questions about your writing partner's paper.
   a) Suggest a different way to travel, using at least two of the given methods.
   b) Ask one question about why something happened.
   c) Suggest one surprising or exciting event to add to the story.

2. When you get your partner's comments, read them carefully. Keep these ideas in mind as you think about your story:
   a) What suggestions for change and improvement do you find in your partner's comments?
   b) Do you reject any of your partner's advice?
   c) What new ideas come to you about your story?

Go on to  Activity 2K

Editing and Proofreading Your Adventure

These travellers have had three very different adventures. You may also have done different kinds of planning and writing so far, depending on which adventure you chose. Now you may finish your story by taking the same steps as everyone else. You have reached the stage of editing and proofreading.

Activity 2K Me — An Editor?

1. Show your writing partner the revised draft of your story.

2. Ask your partner to read your story aloud to see if he or she can find any of these problems:
   a) Are there any misspelled words?
   b) Are there any sentences that do not start with a capital letter or end with a period?
   c) Are there sentences that should end with a question mark, but don't?
   d) Can you find any places where quotation marks are missing from the speeches made by people in the story?
   e) Have capital letters been left off the names of places or people?

3. Use your partner's advice to make corrections to your revised draft. But remember, you have the choice of using or not using your partner's suggestions about your work.

Publishing and Sharing Your Adventure

The final stage in the writing process is sharing your finished writing with someone else. You may publish your story in many ways. This next activity will give you some ideas about how to do this.

Activity 2L   Sharing My Adventure

Choose one of these ways to share your story. Or think of some other ways in which you can get someone to read what you have written.

1. You and your writing partner can read your stories aloud to the members of another writing team.

2. Your class can set up a sharing session at which everyone exchanges stories with other students or reads them aloud to the class.

3. Your class can publish a writing booklet.

4. Each adventure may become a separate chapter of a book containing all the stories written about that adventure.

5. Your class can make a bulletin board display of the stories.

6. Your class can invite a guest to attend a story reading in class.

7. You can read your story to a child in an elementary class.

8. You can mail your story to someone you know and ask that person to comment on it.

A Review of the Writing Process

You have travelled on an imaginary journey in this chapter — the journey of your story. You also took a journey of a different kind — a journey through the stages of the **writing process**. This is a very real journey, one that you will travel again and again throughout this book.

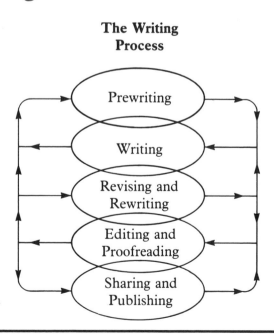

The Writing Process

- Prewriting
- Writing
- Revising and Rewriting
- Editing and Proofreading
- Sharing and Publishing

LINK 3 A

Study this cartoon. Use these questions for a class discussion:

1. What is the humour in this cartoon?

2. Would the cartoon be humourous if the diploma on the wall read *animal psychologist*?

3. What do you think these adults say to the child psychologist?

4. Try your hand at designing a cartoon like this one.

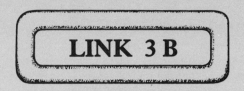

LINK 3 B

This activity will test to find out how good you are at *looking* and *really seeing* what you are looking at:

1. Two members of the class stand at the front of the classroom.

2. Two or more students are chosen to be *it*.

3. Students who are *it* look carefully at the students who are standing at the front of the classroom.

4. The students who are *it* leave the classroom.

5. Each student at the front of the classroom may make up to three changes about themselves.
   Examples: Change the part in your hair; remove your ring and place it on a different finger; change watches with one of the other students at the front of the room.

6. The students who are *it* return to the classroom. They examine the students at the front to find out what they have changed.

Discussion: After playing several rounds of this game, do you become better at noticing the changes? Why?

Of what value to a writer is a good memory for detail? How can you make use of this skill in your next writing assignment?

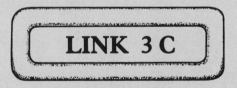

LINK 3 C

"What should I do to become a writer?" Ralph Gray, editor of *National Geographic World*, answered this way:

First, you must be sure you really want to be a writer. If you do, you could already be on your way. But you'll need practice to be good. Look for opportunities to write firsthand accounts of things you have seen or know about. Describe scenes and actions so clearly that people will know exactly what you mean. Don't waste words or try to use big ones. Do a lot of reading on your own and you'll see that simple writing is the best writing. After you finish each piece of writing, read it over as if you were the reader instead of the writer. Does it make sense? Are you sure of your grammar and your spelling? If checking grammar and spelling bores you, then maybe you don't want to be a writer at all.

National Geographic World, June, 1982,

Write answers to these questions in your notebook:

1. Do you like to write? Why or why not?

2. Would you like to become a writer? Why or why not?

3. Do you know anyone who writes as part of his or her job? What do they do?

4. How do you go about writing? Do you like to write at school? at home? where it's quiet? noisy? in pencil or in ink? on lined paper or unlined paper? white paper or coloured paper?

5. Share some of your ideas and thoughts in class.

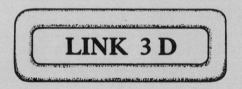

LINK 3 D

This dictation passage reviews the use of capital letters:

The Loch Ness monster is not unique. Many reports of similar monsters have come from all over the world, and one of the best-known of these is Ogopogo of Okanagan Lake. The lake is set on the Pacific slopes of the Rocky Mountains, in Canada's west coast province of British Columbia. The local Indians knew and feared the lake monster or demon; they called him by many names and had many stories and legends about him. When white pioneers came to settle the area, they learned about the lake demon from the Indians, but they also saw him for themselves.

Mary Moon, *Ogopogo*

LINK 3 E

To be a good listener, you have to concentrate on the message the speaker is sending you. This activity gives you practice in concentrating on the speaker's message.

1. Your class will divide into two relay teams.

2. Working alone, think of a direction you can give your opposing player, and write it in your notebook.

Example: Tap your right knee three times, point twice to the ceiling, and stand on your toes with your left hand pointing toward the south. Your directions should not contain more than three actions.

3. The relay works this way:
   a) The first student on Team I reads his or her directions.
   b) The first student on Team II listens to all of the directions and then performs them in correct sequence.
   c) The first student on Team II reads his or her directions to the second student on Team I, and so on. Finally the last student on Team II reads directions to the first student on Team I.

4. One point is awarded for each sequence of directions that is followed correctly. The team with the greater number of points at the end of one round of play wins. (Your teacher may deduct points from a team that does not provide clear directions.)

Variations: One student or a group of students could make up the directions. Then team members pull their directions out of a hat. Or this activity could be performed by groups, with one group of students making up directions and giving them to another group. Students should then make up group directions. For example, they could write something like this: ''One member puts his finger on his head, while two other members jump up and down. Another member pantomimes the reading of her English textbook.''

Au clair de la lune Alfred Pellan

CHAPTER 3

JUST BETWEEN YOU AND ME

IT ONLY HURTS WHEN I WRITE

Try the Painless Journal Technique

Many people think that the two most painful parts of writing are getting started and getting finished. This chapter contains some suggestions about painless ways to start writing. They involve keeping a journal.

Each time you write, you go through the **stages of the writing process**. At times you want to spend more time on some stages than on others. For example, the prewriting stage may take up a great deal of time. Gathering ideas before you write can be a big job. Your journal can help you to keep track of your ideas.

Many writers keep journals to gather ideas. They develop the habit of writing regularly in their journals. This chapter will show you how to set up a journal and gather ideas to use later in your writing. Using a journal is a little like putting money in a bank. You can keep your money in the bank and draw it out later when you need it. In the same way, you can *bank* your ideas in your journal and save them until you are ready to write.

What a Journal Might Look Like

If you found a lost notebook, you might feel curious about the owner and start to read it. What would you think if you read this entry?

Monday

I was afraid this would be the worst day I ever spent in school, and it was. Even worse than the first day of kindergarten. At least then I enjoyed recess and the cookies. Today all I could look forward to was lunch time. That meant spending an hour sitting by myself in a crowded cafeteria. When it's your first day in a new school in a strange town, you can't count on seeing many friendly faces.

Too bad my parents were so keen about taking those new jobs. They could have thought about whether or not I wanted a whole new life.

Tuesday

Another great day. The Math class I'm in is two chapters ahead of where we were at home. I've got to do extra work to get caught up. That was just the beginning. If I made a list of what went wrong today, it would look like this:

1. Left my lunch at home.

2. Tried to ask about phoning home to get my lunch. Forgot my teacher's name and my new phone number.

3. Got lost trying to find the telephone.

4. Tripped on the hall carpet and fell down the main stairs.

5. Had to go to the office to report the accident on the stairs and forgot the principal's name when I got there.

There's no way recess and a snack could make up for this!

Wednesday

The best part of the day was getting a card from Chris this morning. The worst part was how much I missed everybody after I read it. My parents said that if I work hard, they'll let me go back home over the holidays to visit. Only nine weeks to go!

I know one person now at this school—my locker partner. Sharing a set of shelves isn't exactly a lifelong friendship, but at least I had somebody to sit with in the cafeteria today. Kind of a quiet person without Chris's sense of humour, though.

Friday

I made it—the first week in a new school! This weekend I'm going to write and tell Chris all about it. After school, I managed to get from my locker to the front door without getting lost. In fact, it seemed simple. Maybe what they say is true — there's nothing like travel to broaden your horizons!

What a Journal Means

You soon realized that this notebook is really a journal in which the writer is keeping a daily record of events. The idea of keeping a journal is many centuries old. The English word *journal* is borrowed from the French *journal*, meaning *daily*, which goes all the way back to a Latin word *diurnus*, meaning *daily*.

People write in journals for many different reasons. Their journals may be as different from each other as the writers' reasons for keeping them. Often, a journal is personal and private. The writer may not plan to share the journal with anyone else. Because it is possible that no one else will read what has been written in the journal, the writer may be free and informal.

Activity 3A   Thinking About . . .

After reading the journal entry on pages 48 and 49, answer the following questions in your notebook. Be ready to discuss your answers in class.

1. Why might a person keep a journal like this?

2. Who does the writer plan to share this journal with?

3. How do you know whom the writer plans to share the journal with?

4. For each day's journal entry, state one thing that the writer should change before giving it to someone else to read.

5. State one thing that you learn about the writer's personality by reading the week's journal entries.

A Different Kind of Journal

A second notebook contains the following entries. This writer seems to be using the journal in a different way from the first writer. Read these entries carefully.

Took the bus downtown on the weekend. Sat behind a lady and her teenage daughter. They were talking about how they were going downtown to pick out a dress for some party the girl was going to. First step—they got into a squabble over what colour the girl's new dress should be. Next—a fight over whether or not it should be a fancy party dress. Then a real war over what kind of party it was going to be and how the mom didn't like the girl who was giving the party. By the time the bus stopped at the mall, the mom had grounded the girl so she couldn't go to the party anyway. The girl started to cry. Wonder how it sounded when the mom told it to the girl's dad? Not the way it sounded when the girl told her friend, I'll bet. Maybe a good idea for a story?

A good line from a song I heard today: "You can't play life like a video game, because somebody's always changing the rules."

Basketball practice today. Afterwards, the coach talked to us about the game tomorrow. "I don't want you to work too hard trying to be good losers. I don't mind bad losers. As far as I'm concerned, good losers are just people who get into the habit of losing regularly." Never thought of it that way. What would happen to "sportsmanship" if everybody thought that way?

Activity 3B   Planning to . . .

After reading the second journal, answer the following questions in your notebook. Be ready to discuss your answers in class.

1. Why might a person keep a journal like this?

2. Does the writer plan to share the journal with anyone else? How do you know?

3. For each day's journal entry, state one thing that the writer should change before giving it to someone else to read.

4. State one thing that shows that the writer plans to make changes before giving the writing to someone else to read.

Activity 3C   Comparing Journals

Look back at the two journals and answer these questions in your notebook. You should be ready to talk about your answers.

1. Explain one way in which the two journals are alike.

2. Explain one way in which they are different from each other.

3. Explain whether or not the two writers have the same reason or different reasons for keeping their journals.

KEEPING A JOURNAL

The "How-to" of Journal Writing

From the two journals you have looked at, you can see that journals can be set up and used in many different ways. These differences may cause you to ask several questions about keeping a journal.

Why?

- to record daily events
- to keep track of facts and details
- to note interesting observations about people
- to record memories of special or significant times
- to express private hopes and fears
- to explore your feelings about personal experiences
- to form opinions
- to store up creative and imaginative ideas
- to use for prewriting warm-up

Where?

- in a special notebook you carry with you
- in a bound journal book or diary you leave at home
- in a separate section of your English notebook
- on cards or sheets of paper that you save in a writing folder or file
- on anything that you like as long as it helps you keep track of your ideas

When?

- at the same time each day, maybe just before bed or first thing in the morning
- as part of your English class
- when inspiration strikes with a good idea or when you feel creative
- when you want to express strong feelings about something
- when you want to save an idea to use later
- when you need to tell something to somebody
- when you have a question, a joke, a complaint, an idea for an invention

What?

- times that are happy, sad, shocking, surprising, upsetting, or otherwise important to you
- descriptions of special or unusual people
- interesting words
- intriguing ideas
- questions you want to ask or answer
- facts about something you have to write about
- anything else that matters to you

Who Writes Journals?

- professional writers
- travellers
- students
- artists
- people with problems, special projects hobbies, and interests
- me
- you
- anybody at all

Keeping a Journal — How to Get Started

Try to keep a journal of your own. Here's some advice about how to do it:

- Choose a special journal notebook or set aside a part of your English book.
- Set aside a certain time each day to write in your journal, perhaps during class or in the evening.

Activity 3D   Every Day for a Week

1. Try keeping a journal to record events in your own life over the next week.

2. Write down at least one unusual or interesting detail each day about the people, places, or happenings in your life.

Activity 3E   Your Journal Becomes a Word Bank

Use your journal to store up words in a word bank.

1. Make a list of all the nouns you can think of to name the things you would expect to see in a horror movie, in a pet shop, in a video games arcade, or in some sports activity.

2. Make a list of all the verbs you can think of to describe the actions you would expect to take place at a track meet, at a school dance, on a crowded street, or at a fast-food store.

3. List as many words as you can that might be both verbs (actions) and nouns (things).

4. Listen to people talk for one day — your favourite TV programs, a radio dj, your parents, your friends, anyone. Make a list of the interesting words and phrases they use.

5. Think of other ways to add words to your journal word bank.

Activity 3F   The Journal of an Imaginary Person

Here's another way to keep a journal for one week.

1. Choose an imaginary character, for example a servant in Dracula's castle, a cartoon character, or a visitor from another planet.

2. For one week, keep the journal that this character might write.

3. Make up a list of words associated with your character and write them in your journal.

JOURNALS ARE FOR WRITING

How can you start writing painlessly? One suggestion is to develop the habit of writing in your journal regularly. Your journal will become a bank of ideas for you to draw on. You can use it to look back over your record of the important people, places, and events in your life. These things will give you a head start at the prewriting stage of the writing process.

Your Journal and the Writing Process

Your journal is an excellent way to do prewriting for your writing assignments.

Films		Watching
Books		Reading
Music		Listening
People	→ PREWRITING STARTERS ←	Thinking
Pictures		Doing
Animals		Feeling
Objects		Talking
Actions		Imagining

Save your ideas in your journal
and use them as you
go through the other stages
of the writing process.

WRITING

REVISING AND REWRITING

EDITING AND PROOFREADING

SHARING AND PUBLISHING

Activity 3G   Your Journal and Writing

Use one of your one-week journals as prewriting for one of these writing tasks.

1. Reread the journal entries that you made for Activity 3D. Pick out a highlight from the week's events. Write some more about it so that you can share this event with others.

2. Have another look at the word bank that you created in Activity 3E. Choose ten of the best words or phrases that you find in your lists. Put these words together in a paragraph that you can share with others.

3. Reread the journal entries you made for your imaginary character. Write about one event that happened to this character during the week. Prepare this writing so that you can share it with others.

4. Use your journal entries about your imaginary character to find out exactly what kind of person he or she is. Then, use this information to write about what happens when this character meets with the Prime Minister of Canada or some other famous person.

Hooked on Journals

Now that you have started to write a journal, you may want to keep it up. After a few weeks or months it is interesting to see what things concerned you in the past. Perhaps some day you may notice an old notebook on your bookshelf, pull it out, and find it is the journal you wrote as a teenager.

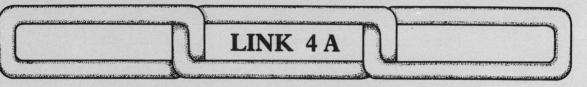

LINK 4 A

Susan and Craig are putting on makeup. They are about to go on stage to perform for an elementary school audience.

1. Imagine that you are either Craig or Susan.

Saskatoon Star - Phoenix

2. In your notebook, write down what you are thinking about at this particular moment. You should be able to come up with eight or ten sentences.
3. Form groups of five or six students. Make certain that about half of the group has written as Craig, and the other half, as Susan.

4. Share your writings as a group.

Now you have a lot of information about Craig and Susan—about what they are doing and what they are thinking.

5. As a group, compose an **imaginary journal entry** for either Craig or Susan. This journal may cover one or two days. Use the ideas that have appeared in your writing, and find new ideas within your group. Your journal entry should be at least one page.
   a) Have one member of the group act as the scribe or writer, while the other group members contribute ideas.
   b) Select one member of your group to read your journal entry to the class.

6. Form a class committee to collect journal entries from all of the groups.

7. Ask the committee to put together all of the journal entries to make up a story about these two young people.

Extension:

1. Talk about the techniques of photography.
   a) Why has the photographer used the reflection in the mirror?
   b) In what other ways could the photographer have shot this picture?
   c) What interesting shots of your school might you take by using this same technique?

2. Talk about the relationship between writing and photography.
   a) How can you use photographs in your journal?
   b) In what ways are writing and photography the same?
   c) In what ways is writing like a photograph that is reflected in a mirror?

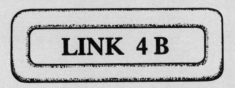

LINK 4 B

In the last chapter, you considered journals and practised journal writing. **Legends** are very much like journals. They are stories handed down from one generation to the next. Each storyteller adds his or her own ideas to the story. This dictation passage gives you information about Inuit legends.

Eskimo story tellers hand down the legends and folk tales of their people from one generation to the next. Like all good story tellers, they often include their own experiences as they relate the tales they heard from others. While most stories are specific to one region or another, many great legends are common to Eskimos throughout the whole Arctic. Eskimo stories give us a glimpse of the way Eskimos live, of their beliefs and ideas, and of their cold barren land.

Ronald Melzack, *The Day Tuk Became a Hunter*

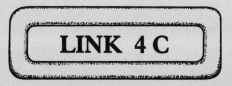

LINK 4 C

Most writers are good observers of the world around them. Sometimes they include in their poems lists of things that they look at or think about. In this example, Johnny Burke, a Newfoundland writer, lists everything that was set out for the party at Kelligrew's Soirée:

There was birch rine, tar twine,
    cherry wine and turpentine
Jowls and cavalances,
    ginger beer and tea;
Pigs' feet and cats' meat
    Dumplings boiled in a sheet
Dandelion and crackies' teeth,
    At the Kelligrew's Soirée.
Johnny Burke

1. In your journal, make up lists of things around you. Here are some starters:

   • things you like to eat at a special party at your house
   • things you like to do on Saturday morning
   • things you see on your way to school
   • the silliest or stupidest things you can think of

2. Choose the list you like best. Arrange the words from this list on a blank piece of paper.

3. Add one or two sketches on the page with your arranged list. Presto — a poem!

A Meeting of School Trustees Robert Harris

CHAPTER 4

WHAT DID YOU SAY?

"Car, cat, dog," says the eighteen-month-old child. "Go out car," says the two-year-old.

Your speaking skills have changed a lot since you were a toddler. You are now required to speak in more formal situations, standing in front of other people.

This chapter will give you some help with this problem. In this chapter you will:

- learn some tips on speaking in front of others
- practise speaking extemporaneously (This means without prepared notes, "off the top of your head".)
- learn how to participate in a discussion

EXTEMPORANEOUS SPEECH

Speak in Front of Everyone? I Couldn't!

Almost everyone feels nervous the first time he or she speaks in front of a group. It doesn't do any good to tell you that, however — who cares what everyone else feels while your knees are shaking?

Three tips may help you:

- **Start.** When you stand up, open your mouth. You will feel foolish (and look like a dying fish) if you don't say anything. So you will be forced to speak. Many speakers report that speaking becomes easy once they get started.

- **Commit yourself to it.** Don't avoid it or postpone it, thinking it will get easier as you get older. Each time you avoid anything, you learn to give in. In the long run you will have to learn to do hard things. Force yourself to speak.

- **Concentrate on what you have to say.** If you start thinking about your sweaty hands, pounding heart, flushed cheeks, and nervous voice, you have no time to think about your message and so you stumble. These symptoms will go away as you talk if you ignore them.

Speaking of Pajamas, the Other Day I . . .

As a working adult, you will do most of your speaking extemporaneously — without advanced preparation. Your boss will come up to you and say, "Tell me about the EDUTEXT computer project." You will mentally summon facts from the information stored in your brain — your data bank — and you will construct the best, briefest, and most organized oral presentation you can.

In the next activity, you will use your past experience and data bank to speak extemporaneously.

Activity 4A   Out of the Hat

1. Your task will be to speak for sixty seconds on a topic drawn from a hat. The topics have been chosen because you know much more about them than you could say in sixty seconds (although you may not feel like that when you pull out your topic).

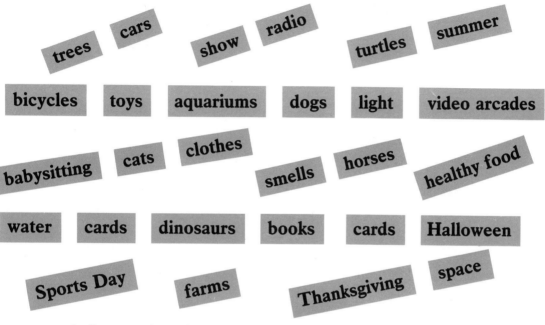

2. Some students in your class will be asked to write each of the suggested topics on a small index card.

3. While this is happening, the rest of the class can brainstorm additional topics to put on index cards. Remember, the topic must be one you feel is within the experience of everyone in the class.

4. Put all the cards in a hat or some other container.

5. Your teacher selects the first student to come up and pull a card. Thereafter, each student may select the next speaker as long as that student has not yet spoken.

6. The rules are these:
   - The stopwatch starts whenever you start to speak, and stops whenever you stop.
   - You must speak for sixty seconds.

Imagine you have drawn the word *horses* as your topic. Some tips to help you if your mind goes blank are:

- **Spell your topic.**
  H - O - R - S - E - S

- **Talk about the different types of your topic.** You probably know several types of horses and what they are used for.

- **Explain how your topic works**— its parts, its colours. Spend some time on the mane, tail, hooves, horseshoes, forelock, eyes, or neck of the horse.

- **Talk about the history of the topic.** Here it would help to explain how people have domesticated the horse and used horses for different purposes. The introduction of horses into North America would be interesting, as would mythical horses such as Pegasus, a winged horse, or the unicorn.

- **Tell an interesting story about your topic.** You may have once failed in an attempt to ride a horse, or had a friend bitten by one, or been to the horse races, and so on.

Talk It Out

To practise speaking extemporaneously, a game called *Talk It Out* is useful.

Activity 4B   Speaking Extemporaneously

1. Divide yourselves into pairs and sit facing each other.

2. Your teacher will announce a topic from the list below and one member of the pair may speak extemporaneously for sixty seconds.

3. Whenever the first speaker stops speaking for more than six seconds the second member of the pair starts.

4. The second member of each pair may not repeat anything the first member said.

5. Keep going back and forth until the teacher says, "Stop" at the end of sixty seconds.

6. The winner is the one still speaking.

7. Try the next topic.

toothpaste

sandwiches I have known

windows

My favorite books

nursery rhymes

edible animals

rafts

children's television

flying saucers

ice cream

running shoes

Well, Yogi Bear is a cartoon of low artistic merit, in my opinion. The only part of the bear that moves are his feet. And the background is just dragged past. They use the same backgrounds over and . . .

My favourite cartoon is the Roadrunner. I love Wily E. Coyote. He's so pathetic — fails every time. And he's so determined — he hatches one scheme after the other. And he's so wonderfully naive — falls for the . . .

Just a Minute

On the British radio show called *Just a Minute*, six very well-educated contestants are given a topic such as *the digital watch*. The first begins to speak: "The Venus de Milo is like the digital watch in that neither has arms."

The object of the game is to try to be the one speaking when the sixty seconds are up.

A variation on *Just a Minute* might be fun for your class, though producing such a clever opening line extemporaneously requires a good deal of experience.

Activity 4C   Playing Just a Minute

1. Divide yourselves into teams of five.

2. Appoint one of your team as a judge. The other four become two teams, each with two members.

3. Use a list of topics such as those following.

4. The judge announces the topic, names the first speaker for the first side, and starts a mental count of sixty seconds.

5. The speaker continues to speak continuously until there is a *challenge* from the opposing team.

6. A member of the opposing team may say, "Challenge," at any time. If one does, the judge writes down what second has been reached and asks, "What challenge?"

7. There are three possible types of challenge:
   a) *Deviation*, which means the speaker has gone seriously off the topic.
   b) *Repetition*, which means the speaker has repeated something. The challenger must say what was repeated.
   c) *Pause*, which means a pause lasted for more than four seconds.

8. The judge decides if the challenge is a good challenge. If the judge upholds the challenge, the challenger becomes the next speaker. If not, the original speaker continues. The count toward sixty seconds is resumed.

9. You can earn points in two ways:
   a) A successful challenge is worth one point.
   b) Being the speaker speaking when sixty seconds are up is worth two points.

10. After fifteen minutes, the person with the most points in each team goes to the finals against representatives from other teams. The rest of the class becomes the audience.

GROUP DISCUSSION

You and your friends often have conversations. You talk with each other and joke back and forth. A discussion is something different.

Why Discuss?

A discussion is a more difficult form of speaking than a conversation because the members of a group have to know a lot about a topic in order to discuss it.

Discussion is a valuable and interesting way to explore ideas on a topic from many different points of view.

You will have a chance to engage in a discussion. But before you start, there are a few things it is useful to know about discussing in groups:

- A good discussion group has either three or five members.

- All members of a discussion group should face each other. Turn your desks so that your backs are toward people from other groups.

- If the purpose of the discussion is to collect information, ask at least one person to be the **recorder** and to take notes.

- Decide on a **chairperson** who will report your results to the class. The chairperson should be someone who speaks fairly well and can remember what was said. Discuss your choice if necessary—the rest of the class will find out about your group from your chairperson, so your choice is important. The chairperson also controls discussion within your group, tells you when to move on to the next question, indicates who will speak next, and asks questions to clarify points.

- Usually you begin by brainstorming the sorts of questions that should be asked about the topic. However, because this chapter is introducing the idea of discussions, some starter questions have been provided for the first few discussions.

- Discuss each question completely before going to the next question.

- List lots of examples. Try to establish some kind of generalization from your examples. For example, your topic might be soft drinks and your first sub-question might be: Should schools be allowed to sell soft-drinks? You would list all the reasons for and against it and then you might establish as your generalization that "Our group has sixteen reasons against schools selling soft drinks and four reasons for it, but we still wanted to have soft drinks sold in school. We finally decided that the strongest reason against it was that primary students are too young to decide for themselves if they want to be fat with rotten teeth."

Activity 4D   Family Rules

For this first discussion, step-by-step notes and a list of discussion questions are provided.

1. Form groups of three or five.

2. Select a recorder.

3. Select a chairperson who will report your group's results to the whole class.

4. Your topic is *family rules*.
   a) What family rules do the people in your group have?
   b) How many family rules do the people in your group have in common? For example, does everyone have some kind of curfew? Do you have to tell your parents or guardian where you're going?
   c) What family rules occur in only one family?
   d) How are family rules set?
   e) What are the punishments for breaking family rules, if any? Which work best?
   f) Are the family rules the same for all brothers and sisters?
   g) What kinds of behaviour are family rules designed to promote?

5. After a specific time limit your chairperson will report your group's results to the class as a whole. Each chairperson should report the general experience of most people in his or her group but also report interesting exceptions.

Activity 4E My Group Was . . .

It is worthwhile to take a few minutes to look at how your group functioned. Try to establish reasons for setting up a discussion in a formal way. Provide written answers to these questions.

1. Why does a good discussion group have three or five members? Why not two? Why not more than five? Why odd numbers?

2. Why should group members face each other?

3. Why is it important to break the topic down into a series of questions?

4. Why were you given a topic rather than being asked to make one up yourself?

5. Why have a recorder?

6. Why have a chairperson? Why shouldn't the recorder be the chairperson?

7. Why were you asked to make a list of examples and then to establish a generalization?

8. Why were you asked to completely exhaust discussion on one question before going on to the next one?

9. Why were you asked to report to the whole class through your chairperson?

Using a Discussion in Writing

In this chapter it has been suggested that a discussion is a good *prewriting activity* because it gives you a broad base of information before you write.

You now have enough information about your opinion on a topic related to family rules. Your opinion comes from your thoughts and ideas about a topic. It is not necessarily based upon facts, but it is drawn from your own judgment and beliefs about a topic.

A simple but clear structure for your opinion would be to:

- state your opinion
- back it up with examples and explanations
- draw a conclusion

Activity 4F In My Opinion. . .

1. Write an opinion on one of the following topics:
   a) The best family rule I know is. . .
   b) The best way to establish a family rule is. . .
   c) The types of punishments that work best for breaking family rules are. . .
   d) There are three common family rules established for the same reasons . . .

2. Find a writing partner and exchange papers. Help each other improve by doing the following things with your partner's written opinion:
   a) Check to see if the opinion is clearly stated at the beginning. Underline it.
   b) Check to see if there are at least three explanations or examples to back up the opinion. Number them.
   c) Is there a conclusion? Underline it.
   d) Does the conclusion say that same thing that is said in the opening sentence? If it does not, suggest some way for your partner to improve it.
   e) Use the *Copyediting Checklist* from Activity 1H.

3. When you get your paper back, consider your partner's comments, and make any corrections you want to make.

4. Write out the final copy of your opinion paragraph.

Talk, Talk, Talk

In this chapter, you have practised speaking extemporaneously, and you have used that skill in your discussion group. In addition, you've learned how to participate in a discussion and seen how that skill can build a groundwork of information that you can use as a source for writing.

LINK 5 A

Winter Theme No. 7 Jack Shadbolt

Winter Theme is a painting by Jack Shadbolt, a Canadian painter.

1. Study the painting for a few moments by yourself:
   a) What lines and shapes do you see in it?
   b) What do these lines and shapes make you think about?

c) What is your reaction to the painting? Why?

d) How do you evaluate the painting? Do you like it or not? Why?

2. Here is some information about the painter:

   Jack Shadbolt grew up in Vancouver. He later travelled in Europe, where he visited in many port cities. Scenes of the harbour were a normal part of his life. He was fascinated by ships and dinghies, harbours, and piers.

   a) Does this information about the painter cause you to look at his painting differently? Why?

   b) What do you see in the painting now?

3. Harbour scenes are often used on postcards. What is the difference between a picture postcard of a harbour scene and Shadbolt's painting?

4. Construct a thought web in your notebook to organize your thoughts and ideas about Shadbolt's painting. (Note: Directions for the construction of a thought web appear in Link 2 on page 25.)

5. Choose three or four ideas from your thought web. List them in your notebook in complete sentences.

6. Finally, as a whole class, talk about *Winter Theme*. Use the questions in 1 to guide your discussion.

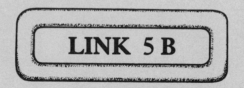

LINK 5 B

This dictation passage was taken from *The Day Tuk Became a Hunter*. Tuk and his family have hidden in their igloo to escape the attack of a fierce bear.

Later that night Tuk crept into the igloo tunnel and gently removed the snow block from the entrance. The ice and snow sparkled in the light of the full moon. Tuk crawled out of the tunnel and quietly began to build a huge snow bank beside it. Once, while he was working, the bear snorted and turned, and Tuk jumped into the tunnel. But he came out again when the bear was quiet, and with his knife he began to carve the snow bank.

Ronald Melzak, *The Day Tuk Became A Hunter*

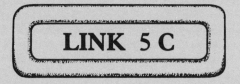

LINK 5 C

The paragraph about Tuk is written in the **past tense**, or past time. That is, the verbs tell you that the action in the paragraph happened in the past. The story is over and Tuk is now a hunter. The author can tell you that the action is over by choosing the past form, or past tense, of the verb. This activity gets you to use number and tense forms of the verb.

Here are some of the common forms of verbs:

Infinitive	Present Tense	Past Tense	Future Tense
to look	I look	I looked	I will look*
to see	I see	I saw	I will see
to sing	I sing	I sang	I will sing

*Note: Sometimes *shall* is used instead of will to signal future tense or time.

1. Make up sentences using *look*, *see*, and *sing* in the present, past, and future tenses. Write these sentences in your notebook.

2. Rewrite the paragraph about Tuk, changing all of the verbs to the present tense.

3. Rewrite the paragraph, changing all of the verbs to the future tense.

4. Rewrite the paragraph once again, in the present tense. But this time add *Tuk and his sister* each time the word Tuk is used in the paragraph. You will also have to make these changes: *he* will become *they*; *his* will become *their*. In other words, when you make the subject of the sentence plural, you often have to change the form of the verb.

A Vision of Animals Kenojuak

CHAPTER 5

I KNOW YOU CAN HEAR ME, BUT ARE YOU LISTENING?

LISTEN! LISTEN! WHAT DO YOU MEAN?

We live in a world full of noise. All day we hear motors running, tires swishing, heaters humming, radios playing, televisions talking, teachers, friends, and parents speaking, and much more. In such an environment it is important to know the difference between **hearing** and **listening**.

In this unit you will:

- learn some good listening techniques
- learn to listen carefully for specific kinds of information
- use your listening skills in a discussion before completing a writing task that outlines an argument

A Listening Questionnaire

The following questionnaire is like many questionnaires you find in magazines. It is not scientifically accurate, but it should help you see what the characteristics of good listeners are.

ARE YOU A GOOD LISTENER?

1. For each of the questions, think back to the last real occasion when the event occurred. Exactly what did you do?

2. If you did more than one, select the one you do most often.

1. When someone is introduced to me, I:

a) look at the person's face carefully and repeat the name to myself

b) use the name in conversation in the next few minutes to try to remind myself of it

c) tend to forget the name and have to ask someone later

d) don't try to remember at all because I may never see the person again

2. When I am phoning someone, I:

a) do other things while listening (flip pages in a magazine, clean out a drawer, write notes)

b) doodle

c) just listen and talk

d) visualize the other person's facial expression while speaking

3. From the last time I heard the news on the radio or TV, I remember:

a) three or more news items

b) two news items

c) one news item

d) nothing but a hazy impression

4. The last time I went into a new room to hear a lesson or a speech, I:

a) sat at the back of the room and whispered to friends

b) sat at the back of the room and listened silently

c) deliberately sat where I would be sure of seeing and hearing the speaker

5. When I am listening to a lecture or talk, I:

a) take notes in my own words

b) take notes in the speaker's words

c) tend to let my mind wander

d) listen carefully

e) mentally argue with or add to what the speaker is saying

6. When I am given instruction, I:

a) write the instruction down

b) listen carefully and go over the instructions in my mind

c) ask a friend later what the instructions were

d) wait until I am ready to start and then find out what to do

7. The last time I didn't understand something I heard, I:

a) asked a question about it

b) asked a friend about it later

c) skipped over it and went on with the rest

d) tried to puzzle it out

Activity 5A   Are You a Good Listener?

1. Read the questionnaire, and then answer each of these questions in your notebook.

2. For each one, record the number of the question and the letter of your answer (for example, 8 a).

3. Check your answer against the answer on the score chart.

4. Record the points next to your answer. For example, if you wrote d for question 1, put one point next to your answer.

5. Total the number of points for the seven questions.

6. Look up your score on the Interpretation Chart.

SCORING

1. (a) 4 points
   (b) 5 points
   (c) 2 points
   (d) 1 point

2. (a) 1 point
   (b) 2 points
   (c) 3 points
   (d) 5 points

3. (a) 5 point
   (b) 4 points
   (c) 3 points
   (d) 1 point

4. (a) 1 point
   (b) 2 points
   (c) 5 points

5. (a) 5 points
   (b) 3 points
   (c) 1 point
   (d) 2 points
   (e) 4 points

6. (a) 5 points
   (b) 4 points
   (c) 2 points
   (d) 1 point

7. (a) 5 points
   (b) 3 points
   (c) 1 point
   (d) 2 points

How did you do? The interpretation chart will give you some idea of your skills as a listener.

INTERPRETATION CHART

30–35 *Excellent listening skills.*
You are an involved person who is interested in the world around you.

24–29 *Good listening skills.*
You try to listen carefully even though you tend to slip up occasionally.

15–23 *Average listening skills.*
Like most people you tend to spend a lot of time hearing rather than listening. As a result your past may be hazy or blurred in your mind by confused impressions rather than a clear recall of events.

7–14 *Poor listening skills.*
You need to make more of an effort to listen carefully. It will not only make you a more enjoyable companion, but it will make your life more interesting.

Hearing and Listening: Is There a Difference?

This chapter is called I Know You Can Hear Me, But Are You Listening? because the two activities, hearing and listening, are the same yet very different. Let's examine this fact further.

Activity 5B   Same and Different

1. **On your own, brainstorm this problem: In how many ways are hearing and listening the same and in how many ways are they different? Write your answers in your notebook, using a chart like this one.**

Hearing and Listening Are . . .

the same	different
1	1
2	2
3	3

2. After five minutes, each person can offer a suggestion to be put on the chalkboard until all ideas are listed.

3. In groups of four or five, decide which are the two most important similarities, and which are the two most important differences between hearing and listening.

4. Each group can report its ideas to the class, explaining its reasoning.

I Know You Are Listening When . . .

There are physical signs that show someone is listening. A baby hears sounds, but until the baby makes sense out of them it is hard to say he or she is listening. Parents are often startled when their ten-month-old, playing in front of the television, suddenly looks up to watch the television. When these babies stop all activity, turn their heads toward the noise, and remain in that arrested position, they show for the first time that they are listening.

Activity 5C   I Know You're Listening

1. With a partner, find the three physical signs described in the preceding paragraph that show someone is listening. Make a note of these on a scrap piece of paper.

2. With your partner, think of all the circumstances when people listen: in conversation, at a dance, on the telephone, passing in the hall . . . Make a note of these on a scrap piece of paper.

3. Working with a partner, make a list in each of your notebooks of all the physical signs that show that people are listening to someone. Use this heading: I Know You're Listening When . . .
   Example: If you say something to friends as you pass them in a crowded hall, you know they've heard if they give a signal such as a nod, or a wave, or . . .

4. On your list, put an asterisk (★) next to the three circumstances in

which you would be most bothered if your friend didn't show that he or she recognized you. Compare your list with your partner's.

Discussion: As a class, list all of the physical signs of listening on the chalkboard. Each pair of students could volunteer one sign at a time until all suggestions are on the chalkboard.

Use this class list to complete the list in your notebook.

Listening for Information

Sometimes when you listen, you have to remember some specific information. This next activity asks you to listen very carefully for some exact information.

Activity 5D   Listening Gets Complicated

1. The class is divided into four teams.

2. Each team is assigned one topic to listen for: *transportation*, *entertainment*, *food*, or *clothing*.

3. The teacher, or one member of the class, reads the list of items slowly.

4. You can only listen; you cannot make notes.

5. When the list is finished, each team member writes out the list as fast as he or she can.

6. Total the number correct on each list. Work out the average of each team, add up the grand team total, and divide by the number of team members.

For example:

6   5   3   1   4   7

will be a grand total of 26
divided by the number in the team, which is 6
to obtain an average team score of 4.33

---

7. The team with the highest average wins.

This is the list to read aloud:

UFO, mozzarella cheese, bikini, longhaul truck, folk singers, bean sprouts, movies, jeep, sweatsuit, avocado, football game, Model-T, sweater, chicken, sundae, rocket, shoulder pads, television, panty hose, lobster, jeans, radio, skiis, bran, Concord jet, skirt, symphonies, milk, parka, singing, station wagon, mittens, stand-up comedian, submarine, space helmet, Volkswagen, reading, nectarine, rock concert.

Listening in the Midst of a Discussion

You are now ready for this discussion, which is designed to help you listen carefully.

Activity 5E   Allowances

1. Move your desks into a large circle.

2. The teacher will choose a chairperson. The chairperson will either select a student with a hand up as the next speaker, or choose someone who has not yet spoken.

3. The first speaker begins with one or two sentences on the topic of allowances.

4. Explore all aspects of allowances: Should you get an allowance? What do you get? What do you get it for? How big should it be? Should it be related to chores? Are you expected to pay for clothes?

5. Each new speaker must re-word what the last two speakers said before adding anything. *"Well, Sally and Jordan both said they get their allowances for keeping their rooms clean and emptying the garbage, but I think that a small allowance with no attached chores actually builds more responsibility because . . ."*

WRITING AN ARGUMENT

You have spent quite a bit of time in this chapter thinking and talking about allowances. In addition to building listening skills, this talk has been the prewriting activity so that you can write a paragraph that presents an argument.

Activity 5F My Reasons Are . . .

1. Select one of the following topics:
   a) the reasons to raise a student's allowance
   b) the reasons to give a student an allowance

2. Follow the system set out in the rest of this chapter as you write your argument as a paragraph.

3. Plan to write this paragraph for an adult reader. How will you have to write for a reader, or audience, such as this?

Activity 5G Getting Ready to Write an Argument

1. On a piece of paper, write down your basic argument. "The best reason to give a student an allowance is to give him or her some independence" or whatever your argument is.

2. Then list as many other reasons as possible to support your argument. Give examples or explanations.

3. Examine your list carefully. Put #1 next to the most important reason, #2 next to the next one, and so on.

4. Use this order to present your reasons:
   • Place your best reason (#1) last.
   • Place your second-best reason (#2) first.
   • Place your weakest reason in the middle.

Activity 5H Writing a First Draft

1. Now write your first draft. Don't be too concerned about mistakes. This is your first draft — just make it legible enough for another student to read it.

2. Select a title for your argument and place it at the top of your writing.

Activity 5I Help Your Partner

Now you are ready to obtain advice on revising your argument.

1. Choose a writing partner. Your partner will try to help improve your argument. Remember, he or she is only an advisor.

2. Use the checklist below to help you look at the arguments.

A Checklist for Helping Your Partner

1. *Conjunctions*
   Circle each *and*, *or*, and *but* in your partner's paragraph.

2. *Sentences*
   Read each sentence in your argument to your partner. But start with the last sentence and read each sentence in order from the end of the argument to the beginning. Mark those that require polishing.

3. *Reasons*
   a) Underline the main words in each reason.
   b) Number each reason in your partner's paragraph. Put an asterisk next to the number if it's explained or has an example.

Activity 5J   Help Yourself

1. Conjunctions: Look at all the *and's*, *or's*, and *but's* circled in your writing. Make a decision about these words. Are they effective? Could your sentences be combined in a different way?

2. Sentences: Improve those sentences that you marked as needing polishing when you read your argument backward.

3. Reasons:
   a) Did your partner mark the same reasons for your argument as the ones you thought you had written? If he or she confused examples for reasons, is there anything you can do to make your argument clearer?
   b) Is there an asterisk next to each number? Can you think of an explanation or an example that would clarify the reasons that do not have an asterisk next to them?

4. Write out a good copy on a clean sheet of paper.

Activity 5K   Send Your Message

1. Send your argument to an adult to get a response to your work.

2. Attach the following letter to your paragraph:

> address
> date
>
> **Dear**
>
> I wrote this paragraph in my writing class. Please read it, then write your response to my ideas at the bottom of this page. Does my argument convince you? What reasons have I forgotten to use? What reasons would prove my reasons are wrong?
>
> Thank you for your help.
>
> Sincerely,

3. Read the response you received from your adult reader. What can you learn from it?

4. Staple your argument and the response together and save them in your writing folder.

Listen, Look, Hear

In this chapter, you have learned:

- information about listening skills
- skill in writing an argument

LINK 6 A

Scorned of Timber, Beloved of the Sky Emily Carr

Scorned As Timber, Beloved of the Sky was painted by Emily Carr, one of Canada's most famous painters. She lived on the West Coast and painted the natural scenery there. This dictation passage describes the intent of her work.

"My paintings do have the real Indian spirit in them," thought Emily. She realized that in the time she had spent sketching them, she had learned much from the Indian people and their art. They had taught her to be bold in her style. It was not important to make a perfect copy of a person or a totem. A perfect copy shows only the outside appearance. You had to probe deeply into the subject and its spirit. Yes, find the spirit and paint with the feeling of the spirit in your heart! Emily had been to England and the United States to study art, but the classes there had not taught her how to paint Canada. It was Canada and her own native people who had taught this to Emily.

Marion Endicott, *Emily Carr: The Story of an Artist*

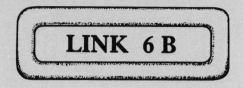

LINK 6 B

Look again at *Scorned As Timber, Beloved of the Sky.*

1. In small groups, talk about your first reactions to *Scorned As Timber.* What do you see in this painting?

2. In your group, consider the title of this painting. What do you think it means?

3. As a group, reread the dictation passage in Link 6 A. Talk about the passage. Tell each other what you think the quotation is about.

4. Use the information from the quotation to look once again at *Scorned As Timber, Beloved of the Sky.* Does the painting suggest the spirit of the British Columbia landscape? If so, how?

5. Look at the paintings in your school. Would Emily Carr think that they are good paintings? Do they get at the spirit of their subject? Talk about your findings in small groups.

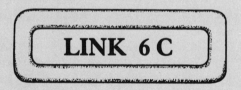

LINK 6 C

One very special kind of writing is the friendly letter. This section will outline for you some of the things you should know about writing a friendly letter.

Explanation: There is a specific way of laying out a friendly letter by convention in North America. A **convention** is a set of rules that everyone follows, not because they are necessarily the best way to do things, but because everyone understands them and knows what to do. For example, the conventional greeting for people in North America is to offer to shake hands and say, "How are you?" while shaking hands. The conventional greeting in Japan is to bring your hands together under the chin, elbows out, and to bow slightly from the waist, head up.

This diagram shows the conventional form of the friendly letter.

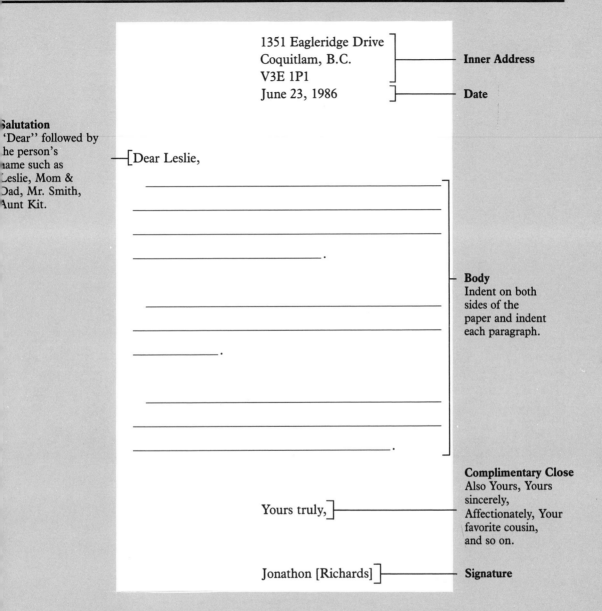

1351 Eagleridge Drive
Coquitlam, B.C.
V3E 1P1 — **Inner Address**
June 23, 1986 — **Date**

Salutation
"Dear" followed by
the person's
name such as
Leslie, Mom &
Dad, Mr. Smith,
Aunt Kit.

Dear Leslie,

Body
Indent on both
sides of the
paper and indent
each paragraph.

Complimentary Close
Also Yours, Yours
sincerely,
Affectionately, Your
favorite cousin,
and so on.

Yours truly,

Jonathon [Richards] — **Signature**

Activity

Try setting up a chart to answer the following questions about the conventions of a friendly letter.

1. **Look at the above letter form and, in your notebook, list and number the parts of the friendly letter.**

2. **What do you think the purpose of each part is?**

3. **Why is each part placed where it is in the letter?**

Conventions of the Friendly Letter		
Convention	**Purpose**	**Reason for location**
1. Inner Address		
2. Date		
3. Salutation		
4. Body		
5. Complimentary Close		
6. Signature		

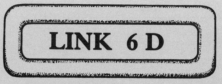

LINK 6 D

In this cartoon, Linus comes up with a novel salutation for a friendly letter.

© 1959 United Feature Syndicate Inc

1. In your notebook, list some different **salutations** that could be used for friendly letters. Place a star beside the ones you take seriously.

2. Make up a list of possible **complimentary closings** that you could use in a friendly letter. Again, star those that you think are good enough to use in a letter.

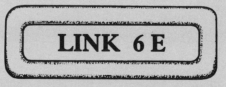

LINK 6 E

It's time now for you to write a friendly letter.

1. Find another class in your school that will read your letters.

2. Send a letter to one of the members of that class — your temporary pen pal.

3. Using the guidelines for conventions of the friendly letter in Link 6 C, write a letter to your pen pal.
   a) Include an anecdote or two of things that have happened in your class.
   b) Choose a salutation and complimentary closing from those that you listed in Link 6 D.

4. Address an envelope for this letter. Directions for addressing envelopes are outlined in Link 6 F.

5. Send your letter. With a bit of luck, you may get an answer and find a friend.

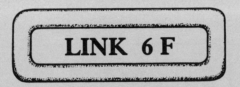

LINK 6 F

The following example shows you the conventions of addressing an envelope.

The **return address** and the **address** are not indented. There is no punctuation at the end of the line except where it is needed for abbreviations.

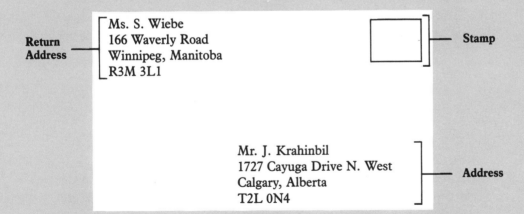

Return Address —
Ms. S. Wiebe
166 Waverly Road
Winnipeg, Manitoba
R3M 3L1

— Stamp

Mr. J. Krahinbil
1727 Cayuga Drive N. West
Calgary, Alberta
T2L 0N4

— Address

Answer the following questions about the conventions of the envelope.

1. For what reason is the stamp placed in the upper right-hand corner?

2. Why is there a return address? Why is it in the upper left-hand corner?

89

3. The return address used to be written on the back of the envelope. Why do you think this convention changed?

4. Why is it usual to use the more formal title of Mr. J. Krahinbil, rather than John Krahinbil, which is probably the way you know him? (Note: it would not be wrong to put John Krahinbil on the envelope.)

5. For what situation might you use the first names or initials of the person you are addressing the letter to, rather than the person's title?

6. Why is the postal code placed on the bottom line all by itself for both the return address and the address?

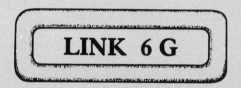

LINK 6 G

Canada has one of the best postal code systems in the world. The Americans have thought of switching their postal code system which is an all-number system, to a combined number and letter system such as ours.

The postal code should be included on each letter for speedy delivery. You can tell roughly where any letter is being sent simply by reading the postal code.

$$\underbrace{\text{V3E}}_{\text{area}} \quad \underbrace{\text{1P1}}_{\text{local}}$$
area designators   local designators

The first three items are called the area designators, the last three the local designators. The first letter represents a province or, in the case of Quebec and Ontario, a part of a province. The letters start with **A** on the east coast and work across to **V** in British Columbia. **X** and **Y** are used for the Northwest Territories and the Yukon.

A   Newfoundland
B   Nova Scotia
C   Prince Edward Island
E   New Brunswick
G
H   Quebec
J

K
L
M — Ontario
N
P

R   Manitoba
S   Saskatchewan
T   Alberta
V   British Columbia
X   Northwest Territories
Y   Yukon Territories

The first number and the second letter designate the areas even more closely. An **O** in the second position means a rural area with no door-to-door postal delivery. The numbers **1** to **9** mean a portion of an urban area. For example, in British Columbia, 3 is a Vancouver number, so V3E 1P1 would be in an area of metropolitan Vancouver, British Columbia.

Activity

1. **What are two reasons why a six-item postal code such as 263 147 is not as useful as a combination of letters and numbers in a postal code such as B6J 1K7?**

2. **What letters have not been used in our postal system? For each of them, why do you think it was omitted?**

3. **Make a list of the postal codes of all the students in your class, and put them on a map of your district.**
   a) **What system is the post office using with the local designators in your area?**
   b) **Check the accuracy of your opinion with the post office.**

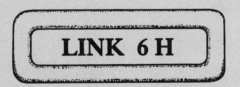

LINK 6 H

Despite the decline in the writing of friendly letters, here is one that is almost compulsory: the **bread and butter letter**. This particular kind of friendly letter is written to thank others for a present, a special trip, a party, or a long visit to their house.

The most important things to remember about a bread and butter letter are these: (1) write it immediately and (2) be sincere.

The form of a bread and butter letter is similar to that of the friendly letter. Here is an example of a letter that Sergei Lamentzji might write to his uncle.

> 158 Fitzroy St.
> Charlottetown, P.E.I.
> C1A 1S1
> July 10, 1987
>
> Dear Uncle Helmut,
>
> Thank you very much for sending me $20 for my birthday. I have been wanting a new catcher's mitt for some time so I rushed out and bought one. I've already used it in a game and we won 16 to 10. Part of that was due to the mitt, no doubt.
>
> Thank you very much for your contribution to our victory.
>
> Your nephew,
>
> *Sergei*
> Sergei

The best way to organize a bread and butter letter is to

- tell the receivers what you are thanking them for
- tell them why you are thanking them
- add a personal note, especially about using or opening the present, and
- add a simple close

Activity

Select any one of the following possibilities and write a good bread and butter letter.

1. You've stayed at a friend's place for the weekend. Write a bread and butter letter thanking your friend's parents for having you over.

2. You received a wonderful sweater as a gift, but it was too small. You exchanged it for another one, slightly different but in your size. Write a thank you letter to the aunt and uncle who sent it.

3. You've received a new book from a neighbour for Christmas. Write a good bread and butter letter thanking him or her.

4. You've received a pair of hand-knit slippers in green and purple from your beloved grandmother, who made them herself. Write a bread and butter letter to her.

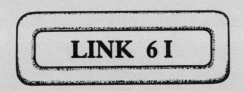

LINK 6 I

In many ways, the habit of letter-writing is a fading art. Canadians use the telephone more than citizens in any other country in the world.

1. Why do Canadians use the telephone more than the citizens of any other country?

2. What advantages does the telephone have over the letter?

3. Can you think of any time in which it would be better to have a letter than a telephone call?

4. Will computers and electronic mail have any effect upon the telephoning habits of Canadians?

5. If electronic mail becomes common, what conventions do you think will be developed for this kind of communication?

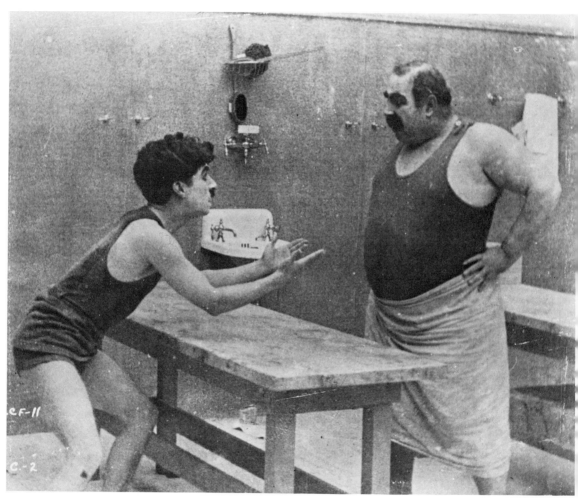

Courtesy of the Museum of Modern Art, New York

Charlie Chaplin facing a masseur in *The Cure*

CHAPTER 6

SIGNATURES ON THE WORLD

MAY I HAVE YOUR AUTOGRAPH?

Let's Go Hunting

Did you know that some people collect signatures? You may keep signatures in an autograph book, or you can become an autograph hunter, buying and selling famous names. Imagine having the autograph of Canada's first prime minister, Sir John A. Macdonald, or pioneer Susanna Moodie — or of Terry Fox or Carling Bassett!

Why are autographs important — and sometimes valuable? For example, you may scurry around on the last day of school each year collecting the signatures of friends in a yearbook. You may stand in line for hours to get the quickly scrawled autograph of a favourite sports star or singer. It's all because autographs are unique. Every time people write their signatures they are giving away something very personal that can be of lasting value.

You Have a Signature Too!

Have you ever thought about your own signature? Write it on a piece of paper. What you see is a little bit of yourself — of who you are — which you can share with someone else. In other words, your signature communicates something. All communication is like a signature saying "Here I am. Pay attention. I have something to tell the world outside of myself."

Let's think about the way you communicate with others around you each day as you make your signature on the world.

Activity 6A   A Short Conversation

Section 1

1. Get a tape recorder for this activity.

2. Find a partner to work with.

3. Read the following conversation out loud. One of each pair of students will be *A* and the other will be *B*.

   A. *Well, how are you? I haven't seen you for such a long time.*

   B. *I'm just great! Guess what? I just won a new ten-speed bike for selling magazine subscriptions.*

   A. *Congratulations! What's your secret?*

   B. *I don't know. I guess I'm just good at getting people to buy magazines.*

   A. *Well, my luck isn't that good.*

   B. *What do you mean?*

   A. *My ten speed was stolen from the school the other day. I had it chained up and everything.*

   B. *How depressing.*

   A. *That's for sure. The police don't know if I'll ever get it back.*

   B. *Anyway, you can ride mine. I'm just on my way to pick it up. Why don't you come along?*

4. When you are comfortable with this short conversation, get two members of the class to volunteer to record it, speaking naturally with appropriate expression.

5. Play back the conversation and listen closely to how expression in the voices adds to the meaning of the words themselves.

6. As a class, discuss how voice expression adds to your daily communication. Perhaps someone in the class can summarize your ideas on the chalkboard.

Section 2

1. Using two more volunteers from the class, play the tape again as these two act out the conversation while the tape is going.

2. Try this again with another pair or two pairs of volunteers. Put your powers of observation to work. As you watch and listen, consider these questions:
   a) What difference does the addition of the actions make to the conversation?
   b) Are there different actions from pair to pair as the conversation is acted out? Why do these differences exist?

3. As a class, discuss these questions and record your observations on the chalkboard.

Section 3

1. Now get two more volunteers to read the conversation in *monotone*. Using a monotone means keeping the same voice pitch and tone of voice — as some computers might talk.

2. Play back the tape and observe two or more volunteers act out this version of the conversation.

3. As a class, discuss your observations. Why is acting out this version more difficult? Record your ideas on the chalkboard.

Section 4

1. Consider now what you have seen and heard during this activity.
   a) In groups of three or four, use the information you have gathered to talk about communication.
   b) Use the following points as a guide:
   - *Verbal communication* refers to communication using words. Which parts of this experiment involved verbal communication?
   - Which part of this experiment involved *non-verbal communication*?
   - Thinking about both the verbal and non-verbal parts of your communication, consider the following:
     What must the *sender* and *receiver* of a message have in common before communication can take place?

2. In your notebook, write your definition of communication and what it involved.

a) Your teacher will ask several class members to write their definitions on the chalkboard.

b) Use these definitions to create a definition that represents the thinking of the class.

c) Write this definition in your notebook under the title, *Communication: Class Definition.*

COMMUNICATION – OUR SIGNATURE ON THE WORLD

Non-verbal Signatures

You have been talking about verbal and non-verbal ways of communicating. People use both kinds all the time to make their signatures on the world. You can communicate with other people as senders and receivers of messages because you share a common understanding of the meaning of the words and the actions that you use.

Have you ever watched old silent movies carefully? Since the actors could not use words to communicate thoughts and feelings directly, they put great emphasis on gesture and facial expression — what some observers of language might call **body language**. These movements and expressions were often exaggerated to make sure that communication was clear.

The pictures that follow are taken from some classic silent films. Remember that these performers had to work solely with their body movements and facial expressions to communicate to the audience.

Activity 6B   Non-verbal Communication

1. Work in small groups of two or three to look at these pictures.

2. Choose one person to act as a recorder. Go around the group and ask each person to suggest what the characters in these movie scenes might be saying to each other and what the story of the film might be about. Each picture is from a separate film, so don't try to fit them together into one story.

3. As a class, share your suggestions of the non-verbal communication of these characters. You may be surprised at the number of possible interpretations of these actions.

Courtesy of the Museum of Modern Art, New York

What emotion is Mae Marsh demonstrating in this photograph from *The Birth of a Nation?*

How are these people using body language?

Tin Type Tangie, 1915.

Non-verbal Signatures Around You

Think some more about the non-verbal part of communication. You may be surprised at how much of the communication that goes on all around you depends on non-verbal means.

Activity 6C   Referees in Action

1. Work in small groups of two or three.

2. In your small groups, study the pictures of the referees in action. For each picture, try to tell which sport is represented and what the non-verbal signal means.

3. Come to a conclusion in your group about the importance of non-verbal communication in sports. Have a recorder write down your group's conclusion as well as some other examples of non-verbal communication in sports that group members know about. See how many signals from various sports, with their meanings, your group members can come up with.

4. Share your conclusions and examples with the rest of the class.

You can see how important non-verbal signals are in sports. If you have ever watched an orchestra play or a choir sing, you know the importance of non-verbal signals in those situations too. The place to observe non-verbal communication all the time, though, is in your daily activities.

Activity 6D   Non-verbal Messages

1. Working with a small group once more, look at the illustrations and talk about what each of the body movements or gestures shown could mean.

2. How definite are these non-verbal messages? If any of the pictures can have more than one interpretation, suggest alternate possibilities.

3. Have a group recorder write down the specific gestures and/or body positions that make up each non-verbal message as group members suggest these.

4. Compare your findings as a whole class. Notice similarities and differences in your observations.

Activity 6E   Sending Non-verbal Messages

1. Form a new work group of three or four students.

2. Take turns in your group to show each other how you would send the following messages using non-verbal signals or body language:

   a) "Don't look now, but the teacher's standing right behind you. Try to ditch the elastic band and spitballs."
   b) "I don't have a clue what you're talking about!"
   c) "Come over and sit down here beside me."
   d) "I'm not going to budge one inch!"
   e) "Please believe me; it's your last hope."

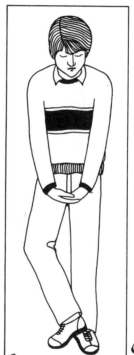

Verbal Signatures on the World

Can you understand this message?

kjngeatsxzugkjzcqjuxgk

This message uses symbols you are familiar with — the letters of the alphabet — but you have just been asked to deal with an unfamiliar arrangement of these symbols. They are coded in a way you do not understand. A code is a system of symbols, such as letters, which have an accepted meaning so that senders and receivers of spoken or written messages can understand one another.

You already know the regular alphabet code, but you will have to work out the message contained in this new system.

Let's break this code. Use this decoding system to help interpret the message in the previous paragraph. Find the letter from the message in the code line. Then, look underneath it in the meaning line to find the letter that you will understand.

code: n a q e b s w d u y f v o g x r h z k j c l i m t p
meaning: a b c d e f g h i j k l m n o p q r s t u v w x y z

When you understand the meaning the sender of the messages has given to each of the symbols, the message becomes clear.

A breakdown in communication occurs when the sender and receiver of a message do not share the same **meanings** for the symbols they use to communicate.

Activity 6F   A Code

1. **Your class should divide into pairs.**

2. **Each pair should make a code based on the alphabet. The code you just worked with is an example of what to do. The sample code you worked with uses letters to represent other letters. You might like to use numbers or symbols you make up yourselves to represent letters.**

3. **Construct a simple message with your code and trade with another pair of students.**

4. **After you have puzzled over each other's messages, supply the *key* to your language code.**

5. **Discuss your experiences as a whole class. How is this experience like the communication that you are involved with every day?**

A WORLD OF SILENT DARKNESS

Helen Keller: How Would She Learn?

In 1882, when she was only seventeen months old, Helen Keller suffered a fever that left her deaf and blind. How would she learn to speak, let alone to read and write? It seemed she was doomed to a world of silent darkness.

Courtesy of the American Foundation for the Blind, New York

Have you ever thought about what people do if they can't use oral and written language? Helen Keller was lucky. Miss Sullivan became Helen's life-long teacher and friend and helped Helen learn to communicate with the world around her.

Activity 6G   The World of Helen Keller

1. Get together with one or two other students in your class and talk about how you would teach Helen Keller to communicate with others.

2. Be sure to write down your ideas in your notebook. As you talk, keep these facts in mind:
   a) Helen was both deaf and blind.
   b) You would have to teach her an alphabet that does not depend on sight or sound.
   c) You would have to teach her to associate words with things — words she has never heard and things she has never seen.

3. As a class, share your ideas and then summarize them on the chalkboard. Now read to find out how Annie Sullivan taught Helen.

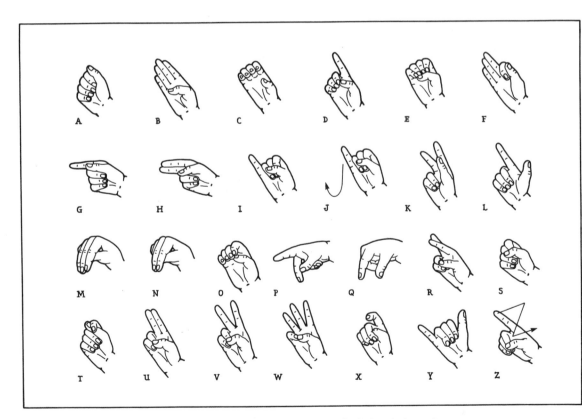

Manual Alphabet used by the deaf of North America

Helen Breaks the Code

Since Helen's sight and hearing were severely damaged, Annie had to use one of Helen's remaining senses, the sense of touch. Annie decided to teach Helen a form of the **manual alphabet**, an alphabet of finger signals. These signals, usually **signed** into the air for deaf people to see, could be pressed onto the palm of Helen's hand. The manual alphabet was invented in France over two hundred years ago. It shows that our spoken and written alphabet can be transformed into something where speaking or writing are not necessary to communicate.

Activity 6H   Signing

1. Refer to the manual alphabet and with a partner, spell out brief messages to each other. You are now learning *signing*. Signing is one more way to make a signature on the world.

Enjoying the World

Some television stations now include **closed captioning** for the hard of hearing—pictures of someone signing the program, or the written text of the program flashed across the bottom of the screen. Just think how such a service opens up the world for many people.

Another language code that opens up the world for a great number of people is Louis Braille's system of raised dots on paper that blind people can *read* with their fingertips. Certain tools also make it possible for blind people to write using this code. Some restaurants now provide menus in Braille.

Activity 6I   Braille

1. With a partner, write down a brief Braille message with ink or pencil dots.

2. Trade messages with another pair of students and decode their message.

3. Try to get an example of Braille to bring to the classroom. Let your classmates see how it feels to read Braille.

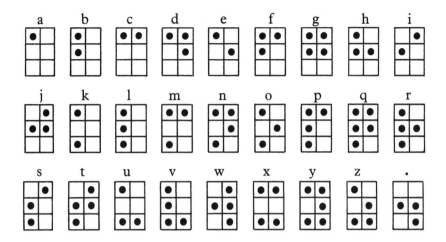

Try to read the following message in Braille.

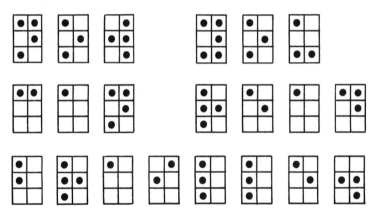

This alphabet is used by the blind to read.

Signing In

Communication is a central part of your life. Without it, you would remain in a world of solitary isolation.

As you can see, you use various kinds of verbal and non-verbal communication codes each day to make your own signature on the world. Although everyone around you uses the same basic codes, your communication pattern is unique—just like your signature. The rest of this chapter will give you a chance to explore this idea as you discover more about your own personal signature on the world.

Activity 6J   My Signature on the World

1. In groups of two or three interview each other about your verbal and non-verbal communication characteristics. Use the box on the next page entitled *My Signature on the World* as a guide for interviewing. When you are interviewing someone, don't forget to keep accurate notes of what is said.

2. When the interviews are complete, give the information to the person or persons you interviewed.

3. When you receive the information about yourself, use it to write about yourself. The focus of your writing will be your own communication, so call it My Signature on the World.
   a) As you write, assume you are introducing yourself to someone you don't know very well.
   b) Organize your material so that you present yourself in an interesting way.
   c) Be sure to write about both verbal and non-verbal communication and how you use them each day.

4. When you have finished your first draft copy, form a small group so you can read each other's work and make suggestions for revision and rewriting.
   a) Can you think of anything that should be added? deleted? replaced with something else? rearranged for a better effect? Make any helpful comments that you can.

5. Write your final draft, using any of the good suggestions from your revision team and making any other changes you think of yourself.

6. Proofread your work carefully to catch mechanical errors (check spelling, punctuation, capitalization). Proofread each other's drafts if you wish.

7. Collect all the Signature on the World pieces into a class booklet for students who will be in this classroom in the future. They will enjoy reading about the "ghosts of the past" who have inhabited this room.

8. Include a class picture or a picture of each class member in your book, if you wish.

My Signature on the World

Interview Outline

1. What are your favourite words or phrases? These can be words and phrases other people use, but which you consider *yours* and which people associate with you.

2. What words, if any, do you pronounce differently from most people around you? Is there any reason you pronounce them differently?

3. What do you think of your handwriting style? Do you write large or small? Straight or slanted? Neat or sprawling? Do you press the pen down hard or let it glide over the page? Do you write quickly or slowly? Is your writing hand steady or shaky? What do you think your handwriting tells you about yourself, about your personality or character?

4. When you are talking, do you use your hands very much? In what way? What other movements, gestures, or facial expressions do you frequently use when you are talking? Are there any gestures or hand motions you use to say *hello* and *good-bye*?

5. What gestures or body movements do you use to express happiness, fear, or surprise? Do you think you use quite a bit of body language or non-verbal communication or hardly any?

6. What do you especially like to talk to people about and to write about?

Signing Out

In this chapter, you have explored some of the principles of verbal and non-verbal communication. You have had the opportunity to consider these things as they relate to yourself as a communicator.

As you have studied communication, you have had a chance to practise communication skills: speaking, listening, reading, writing and viewing. Through your entire life you will be using these skills to help you make your signature on the world.

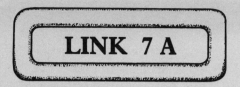

LINK 7 A

The next chapter is about UFOs, so here is an activity to get you thinking about them.

1. In your notebook, construct a thought web, with the word UFOs as the centre.

2. Share your webs in small groups.

3. If you see a word that you like, or hear about a good idea, add it to your own web.

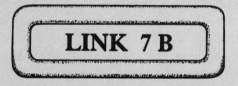

LINK 7 B

People have a special ability to see relationships between things, to look at two seemingly unrelated objects and see the similarities or differences in them. For example, what is the next word in this series: spring, summer, autumn, — — ? Easy, isn't it? Of course the answer is *winter*. You were able to see the relationship among these words.

This question was so easy that you probably didn't think very hard about the answer. Can you find other relationships among these words: *spring, summer, autumn, winter*? Look hard for the unusual relationship.

Here are some other examples of questions in which you can find relationships?

1. What is the missing number:
   a) 1 3 5 7 — 11

   b) — 16 14 11 7 2

   c) 60 55 57 52 54 —

   d) 74 64 — 53 52 42 41 31 30

Discussion: Talk in class about the way you thought out your answers.

2. What do the words in each set have in common? Write your explanations in your notebook.

a)   bat   hockey stick   tennis racquet
b)   newspaper   encyclopedia   library
c)   blood   sap   water
d)   poem   ballet   hockey game
e)   garage   book   airplane
f)   staples   clock   poem

Discussion: Share your answers in class. Do all of the students in your class have the same answer? Why or why not?

How did the different members of your class go about solving these relationship problems? In other words, how did they think through these problems?

People quite often use their ability to see relationships in speaking and writing. You may have heard someone who is angry described as "mad as a wet hen." Or, something that is very hard as "hard as a rock." Those people who are often the most entertaining to talk to or the best communicators, are those who come up with fresh, new comparisons or relationships. Let's look further at the relationships between objects or ideas.

In writing and speaking, this special relationship has a name: *simile.* This diagram shows how this relationship works:

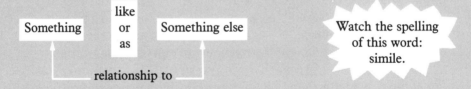

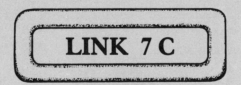

LINK 7 C

1. Choose one of the following **simile starters**.

2. List in your notebook as many similes as you can with this one starter.

3. Make a poster of your similes. Illustrate each simile with a simple sketch. Keep your illustrations simple.

a) as soft as . . .
b) as noisy as . . .
c) as quiet as . . .
d) as happy as . . .
e) as big as . . .
f) as rough as . . .
g) as friendly as . . .
h) as crooked as . . .
i) as crabby as . . .
j) as nervous as . . .

Example

As happy as . . .

. . . A LITTLE KID WITH AN ICE CREAM CONE

. . . A DOG WITH A T-BONE STEAK.

. . . MY PARENT'S AT THE WORLD'S LARGEST GARAGE SALE.

. . . A SAILBOAT IN A STIFF WIND.

LINK 7 D

1. In your notebook, write each of these phrases to complete the similes.

a) — — as/like a Cadillac
b) — — as/like the Atlantic Ocean
c) — — as/like a seagull
d) — — as/like the Trans-Canada Highway
e) — — as/like the CN Tower
f) — — as/like a daffodil
g) — — as/like a comb

2. In small groups, compare answers. Find the three most striking similes among your answers.

LINK 7 E

1. Look for *similes* in the world around you.
   a) For one week, make a list of all the *similes* you hear in talk around you.
   b) Listen to the radio, particularly your favourite disc-jockey, and list the similes you hear. Do the same with your favourite TV program.
   c) Talk about your findings in class. What kind of similes do people use in their speech?
   d) Make a class poster of the examples your class has found. Give it this title: *Similes in the Real World.*

2. Look through several magazines and newspapers.
   a) List the similes that you find in the advertisements.
   b) If you can cut up the magazines, make a collage of these similes in your notebook. Use this title: *Similes in Advertisements.*

LINK 7 F

Here are some similes that were found in comic books.

1. Study these similes.

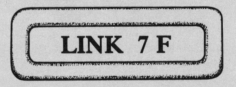

© 1984 Archie Comic Productions I[r]

2. Which one do you like best? Why?

3. Which one do you think is least effective? Why?

Extension: Make a collage of similes found in comics and magazines. Be sure to get permission before you cut them out.

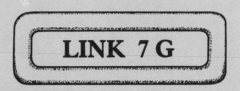

LINK 7 G

In the next chapter, you will have to use your five senses to write description. This activity will help you understand how you can choose words to describe each of the five senses.

1. Think about a hamburger stand. In your notebook, make lists of the things you would see, hear, touch, taste, and smell:

I see	I touch	I taste
I hear	I smell	

2. Form small groups of three or four students. Compare lists. Add to your own list any good words from those in your group.

3. Discuss your lists. For which senses did you find the greatest number of words or phrases? Why? The least number? Why?

4. In ten minutes, write a paragraph about a visit to a hamburger stand. Your description should be written for a person from Mars, who knows nothing about hamburgers. Be sure to choose words that appeal to all five senses.

5. In small groups of three or four students, share your paragraphs by reading them aloud to each other.

Floraison Alfred Pellan

CHAPTER 7

UFOs: OUR SHY VISITORS

FROM DULL TO DAZZLING

The Art of Description

Sometimes the choice of a few words makes all the difference, changing a story from dull to dazzling. The art of making a story come alive often depends on good description.

This chapter asks you to work on using description in your writing. Creating good description means that what you do at the prewriting stage is very important. You should observe as many details as possible. Later on, you can select just the right details to make the reader see and feel what you want. When you feel strongly about your story, you want to make sure that the reader shares your feelings.

Unexplained Visits

For centuries people have been fascinated by the idea of visitors from other planets. Even in ancient and medieval times, people wrote about seeing spaceships or non-human aliens. Today some people also have photographs which they say are pictures of alien ships in Earth's skies.

It is even possible to find cases where people describe being kidnapped by aliens, taken aboard a spacecraft, examined, and released.

Interest in the subject of visitors from other planets quickened about the middle of this century. *Foo fighters*, unexplained balls of light, sometimes followed fighter planes on bombing missions during World War II. Strange rocketlike craft were reported frequently over Sweden in 1946. In 1947, a civilian pilot named Kenneth Arnold reported the flight of strange crescent-shaped craft over the mountains near Mt. Rainier, Washington. Today, similar reports still come from almost every country in the world.

A person who has a story to tell about alien visitors or spacecraft wants to share the experience with other people. The story should include important details about what is happening. Such details paint an exciting picture in words for the reader to enjoy. Using words to paint a picture for the reader is called **writing description**.

Activity 7A   Lights Through the Trees

The following story tells about alien visitors to Earth.

1. **Read the story carefully and then make a list in your notebook of everything it tells you about the situation and the alien visitors.**

2. **Be sure to pick out all the specific facts you can find. Be prepared to discuss your list with other students in the class.**

3. **Keep your list in your notebook. It will help you with another assignment later.**

> A funny thing happened. I was walking along the trail. I saw lights through the trees. I went closer. There was something big near the trail. It didn't look like an airplane. It was sort of flat and round. There were coloured lights outside. A door opened on one side. Several creatures came out. They were holding things. The creatures didn't look like human beings. They moved around for a while. Finally they went back inside.

Activity 7B   The Aliens Have Landed

1. **Study the picture of alien visitors to Earth.**

2. **Pick out all the specific facts you can find by looking at the picture.**

3. **Be prepared to discuss your list.**

4. **Keep your list in your notebook. The facts you observed will help you with another assignment.**

Activity 7C   Two Stories

Look again at the alien visitor story and drawing.

1. Study the picture of alien visitors to Earth.

2. Pick out three places where you think the story leaves out interesting or important details.

3. Describe these places and list the details in your notebook.

4. Discuss your list with your writing partner.

5. Together, look back at the picture and try to fit these details into the story.

6. Make notes in your notebook about where the details would go.

7. Work by yourself to revise and rewrite the story by including the extra details and information you have learned from the picture.

Your revised version of the story should paint a clear and exciting picture with words.

STORIES FROM OUTER SPACE

What do you think an alien creature or a spaceship would be like? The two stories that follow give you descriptions of these things. You do not have pictures to show you what the writers had in mind. They depended on words to describe their subjects. Read the two descriptions carefully, and notice the way each writer uses words to paint a picture.

Description 1

The spaceship seemed to sing as it flashed across the skies. Its powerful engines hummed a strange song about space and stars and faraway places. Spinning like a ball tossed through space, the ship circled the planet. In the crisp air of the Rockies, the autumn stars twinkled, and the ship shone among them like a beacon. Finally it came to rest, hanging in the air above a city.

The ship was so huge that its shadow darkened the streets of the city below. All along the rim of the huge ship were portholes. Lights flashed and glowed through these portholes—green, yellow, blue, and icy white. For a long time, the ship hovered in mid-air, like a monstrous creature making up its mind whether to pounce. Every detail, even the meteor marks pocked in the ship's silver hide, was visible to the people in the city. The engines hummed angrily. Then suddenly the ship whirled through the air and vanished into space as mysteriously as it had come.

Description 2

He bubbled and popped and snorted when he spoke. He twisted and floundered and flopped along the floor like a living rug when he ran.

When he ate, he sucked and slurped. When he sang or laughed, he let out the sort of shrill blast a referee's whistle makes. He was the ambassador to Earth from Alpha Centauri.

Like all members of his race, he reminded human beings of a large, living pancake, sprouting a soft coat of tiger-striped fur. Any human being who measured him would discover that he was about a metre wide but only a few centimetres thick. Set in the very centre of his round, flat body was his disc-shaped head. His face sported a magnificent set of cat-like whiskers on either side of his snout. Somehow, in spite of everything else, what you noticed most was the cold, calculating look in his alert, yellow eyes.

Activity 7D   Descriptions of Aliens

1. From these descriptions, what do you learn about the alien creature and the spaceship?

2. Make lists of four words or phrases that give you information about what each of them is like.

Activity 7E   Feelings About Aliens

1. What feelings do you get about the alien creature and the spaceship?

2. For each one, make another list of two words or phrases that build up that feeling.

Activity 7F   Description Through Comparison

1. Find at least one place in each description where the writer compares the alien or the spaceship to something else.

2. In each case, explain why you think the writer wanted to compare those two things.

Activity 7G Writers' Guidelines

1. What should a writer do to make descriptions interesting?
   a) Make up a list in your notebook of two helpful hints for writers to follow.
   b) To get ideas, you may want to look over your answers to Activities 7D, 7E, and 7F and work with your writing partner.

2. Discuss your list with other students and draw up a class list.

A WRITER'S MAP

What you notice about someone else's writing will often help you with your own. Thinking about the descriptions you read gave you some ideas about how to make your writing as detailed and exciting as a picture. There are ways to do this. The following list tells you about some of them.

Writers' Guidelines

1. **State the facts.** Give information such as facts about the size, shape, and colour of the object you are describing. For example, "Any human being who measured him would discover that he was about a metre wide but only a few centimetres thick."

2. **Put in plenty of action.** Include colourful action words and modifiers. For example, use strong verbs liked "bubbled and popped and snorted." Intensify the action with adverbs, for example, "hummed hungrily."

3. **Show the centre of the actions.** Build up the story with specific, colourful nouns, for example, "snout," "rim," and "beacon." Choose adjectives to complete the picture, for example, "a large, living pancake."

4. **Use your senses.** Let the reader know what your five senses tell you—that is, what you smell, taste, see, hear, or feel. For example, "a soft coat of tiger-striped fur" appeals to your sense of touch and sight.

5. **Make comparisons.** Build a bridge for the reader. Show how something unusual or unfamiliar is a little like something else the reader knows about. For example, "He let out the sort of shrill blast a referee's whistle makes" and "spinning like a ball tossed through space." Sometimes you may describe an object as if it were alive or had human feelings, for example, "The ship seemed to sing" and "The engines hummed hungrily."

REVVING UP THE ENGINE

For your major writing project in this chapter you will be asked to write a story using **description**. What you do at the **prewriting stage** is very important. You should observe as many details as possible. Later on, select the right details to make the reader see and feel precisely what you have imagined. The following activities will help you build up a bank of writing ideas.

Imagine that you have witnessed the landing of an alien spacecraft. The aliens spotted you immediately and have taken you on board their ship. You are amazed by what you see. You want to be sure of as many details as possible because you will use them later when you describe your adventure.

Activity 7H   Get the Facts

1. Study the picture carefully.

2. Make up lists of two facts each to tell about the ship's design, the aliens' appearance, and their activities.

3. Put the picture away.

4. Make up a list from memory of all the facts you can remember, such as the size, shape, and number of the aliens and the details of the ship's construction.

5. Discuss your lists with your writing partner.

6. Together, check your lists with the picture to make sure that your facts are complete and accurate.

Activity 7I Plenty of Action

1. Write down a list of ten interesting verbs (action words) that tell about what is happening on board the ship and put them into groups that tell about certain kinds of action—for example, what the aliens do, what happens when the ship is operating, and what you do.

2. Using your list of verbs, make up a list of adverbs, or words to describe the actions, on a separate sheet of paper.

3. For each verb, choose a word that answers the question *how?* For example, if you picked the verb *roared*, you might pick the adverb *angrily* or *loudly*.

4. Exchange lists of verbs with your writing partner.

5. Using your partner's list of verbs, make up a list of adverbs on a separate sheet of paper that describe those actions.

6. Discuss the results and explain why you made the choices you did.

7. Keep your lists to use for the major writing project in this chapter.

Activity 7J The Centre of the Action

1. Write down lists of colourful nouns that name the things you expect to see.

2. For instance, name three things you would see outside the ship.

3. Give three names for pieces of equipment you expect to find inside the control room.

4. Name three objects the aliens might be wearing or carrying. Use your imagination as well as the picture.

5. Discuss your lists with your writing partner.

6. Do your lists include the same things?

7. Add the nouns for important or interesting things that were not on your list.

8. Using your list of nouns, make up a list of adjectives, or words that describe the things you have named, on a separate sheet of paper.

9. For each noun, choose a word that answers a question like *What kind, colour or shape?* and *How big* or *how many?*

10. For example, if you picked the nown *creature,* you might pick the adjective *hostile* to say what kind and *immense* to say how big.

11. Exchange list of nouns with your writing partner.

12. Using your partner's list of nouns, make up a list of adjectives on a separate sheet of paper.

13. Discuss how the moods or feelings in the two lists are different because of the choices you made.

Activity 7K   Get Your Senses Involved

1. Use your sense of *hearing.* Make lists of two words each that describe the sounds of the ship's engines, the airlock door opening, and the aliens speaking.

2. Use your sense of *touch.* Make lists of two words each that describe the texture of the ship's outside walls, the feel of the floor under your feet, and the temperature of the air inside the ship.

3. Use your sense of *smell.* Make lists of two words each that describe the smell of the air inside the ship, the aliens' food, and a plant inside the ship.

4. Use your sense of *taste.* Make up lists of two words each that describe the tastes of something the aliens gave you to eat and water from the ship's tank.

5. Use your sense of *sight.* Make up lists of two words each to describe the colours inside the ship, the light inside the ship, and the shape of the alien's bodies.

6. Discuss your lists with your writing partner.

7. Which words appeal most strongly to one of your senses?

8. Pick out the weakest list each of you has made, and work together to add strong, colourful details to this list.

Activity 7L   Compare What Happens: Similes

Complete the following statements in your notebook. Each one helps build up the experience you are describing by making comparisons to something else.

The alien creatures' eyes glowed like _____

_____.

The way they were looking at me reminded me of _____

_____.

Their voices were as _____ as _____.

Their skin looked like _____.

Their hands reached out for me like _____.

My heart began to beat as fast as _____

_____.

Activity 7M   Creating Similes

1. Make up your own list of two sentences which use "like" or "as" to make comparisons. They may tell about the ship, the alien beings, or your feelings.

2. Write them in your notebook.

3. You may want to work these comparisons into your major writing project in this chapter.

Since the middle of this century, hundreds of people have reported seeing strange objects in the sky. Sometimes no one can find an explanation for the sight. Such sights are therefore called UFOs or *unidentified flying objects*.

Activity 7N   Put It All Together

This paragraph tells about the sighting of a UFO. The descriptive words and details have been taken out of the paragraph.

1. Rewrite the paragraph in your notebook to build up a good description.

2. Fill in each blank with the kind of word or detail indicated.

In the   (adjective)   air of the Rocky Mountains, the   (adjective) stars   (verb)   like   (simile) . I had set up my camp and was   (verb)   in my blankets, wrapped up as warmly as   (simile) . Suddenly I   (verb)   that one star   (verb)   (adverb)   across the sky, moving as   (adverb)   as   (simile) . I lay   (adverb)   in my blankets as the strange star began to   (verb)   (adverb) . It came closer and closer. I heard a   (adjective)   noise that sounded like   (simile) .

I began to feel strange things happening. The ground started to   (verb) , and every metal object in my camp   (verb)   and   (verb) . The sky was   (verb)   (adverb)   with a   (adjective)   light. Now I could see clearly that the strange star was actually a   (adjective)   (noun)   with   (noun)   and   (noun) . It   (verb)   overhead for a moment. Then it   (verb)   as suddenly as   (simile)   and was gone.

3. **Compare your completed paragraph with your writing partner's.**
   a) **Each of you should point out the best descriptive sentence in the other's paragraph.**
   b) **Pick out the sentence that has the weakest description and suggest other words that could be used to improve it.**

BLASTING OFF: FOLLOWING THE WRITING PROCESS

Now you are ready to use some of your ideas in a descriptive story. Here are two suggestions for story ideas. They both ask you to use description to paint an exciting picture for the reader. Include specific details and interesting comparisons. Choose one of these projects.

Project 1
Seeing the alien spacecraft was a fantastic experience. Now that you are safely home, you have the opportunity to describe the event. Your local newspaper has asked you to write a story giving a detailed description of the spacecraft, the aliens, and your experiences. The editor advises you to make your description as colourful and specific as you can. What you observed was really "out of this world," so you can't count on the readers knowing what you have in mind. Write the descriptive story you would send to the newspaper.

Project 2
Imagine that you are the captain of the alien spacecraft. Part of your job is to write a detailed description of your landing on Earth. This description will be sent to your commanding officers back on your own planet. They want specific details about what Earth and its inhabitants are like. Write the descriptions you would send back to your own planet to tell what you observed when your ship landed on Earth.

After you have chosen one of the writing projects, follow the steps in the writing process.

Prewriting

1. Work with your writing partner to decide what kind of information should go into your writing.

2. Make a list of the topics you would include, such as details about the ship's design and the aliens' appearance, or details about Earth's landscape and human physical features.

3. Check the bank of ideas you built up when you did the activities throughout this chapter and select the most interesting details that fit your topics.

4. Remember your audience for this writing:
   Project 1 — the readers of the newspaper
   Project 2 — your commanding officers.

Writing

1. Write the descriptive story you plan to send to the newspaper or back to your commanding officers. At this stage, you may want to concentrate on using all the details you selected for your story. Do not worry about whether everything is completely correct. You will have the chance to go back and polish your work.

Revising and Rewriting

1. Share the first draft of your story with your writing partner. You can help each other by doing these things:
   a) Ask two questions about something else you want to know in the story.
   b) Point out places where details could be added to appeal to the sense of hearing and the sense of touch.
   c) Suggest one comparison that could help explain how something in the story is like something else.
   d) Point out any sentences that repeat something you have already been told.

2. How good are you at creating pictures with your description?
   a) Exchange your story with your writing partner and read your partner's story carefully. Then try to draw a picture based on the description given in the story. Ask your partner for a clearer description if you are confused or need more details.

b) When you get back your own story and the picture your partner drew, notice any differences between the picture and the scene you had in mind. You may need to make your description clearer or more detailed.

c) Revise your story as needed to include a clearer description. Include extra details which might help the reader to picture the scene.

Editing and Proofreading

1. Exchange your story with your writing partner. Help each other by doing the following.
   a) Point out any verb that could be replaced by a stronger action word.
   b) Point out any place where an adverb could be added to tell the reader how something was done.
   c) Suggest a colourful specific noun to replace one that is too vague or general.
   d) Pick out any place where an adjective could be added to describe the size of something.
   e) Add two words to the story to describe the colours of things.
   f) Pick out any sentence that is unclear in meaning.

2. Make any necessary corrections and write the good copy of your finished story.

Publishing and Sharing

1. Have a sharing session during which you exchange stories with other members of the class.

2. Make a bulletin board display where you post the finished copy of your story along with the picture your partner drew to illustrate the scene.

3. Invite the art class to a display and story session where you show off your class artwork and stories.

In Orbit

The subject of visitors from other planets is fascinating in its own right. However, even a good topic suffers if it is not described well.

In this chapter, you have used the **writing process** to put **description** into your writing. Good description helps make any topic come alive for the reader.

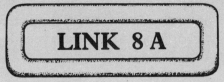

LINK 8 A

"Hi there! A short political message while you're waiting for the walk sign."

1. In your notebook, list at least five places in your world from which **short messages** could be delivered.

2. What kind of messages could be delivered from these places?

Discussion: What might it be like to live in a world like the one suggested in this cartoon?

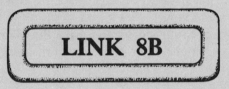

LINK 8B

In the cartoon in Link 8A the exact words of the speaker have **quotation marks** around them. Authors often include exact speech in their writings.

1. Look at this story to review the rules for using quotation marks:

Pavlo quietly pushed the side door open. He was late for school for the third time this month. — exact words of speaker

"Is that you, Pavlo?" A harsh voice echoed down the long hallway. — question mark at the end, inside quotation mark

"Yes, MON-I," Pavlo answered. He had forgotten that the school had installed a new computer to monitor the behaviour of students. — new paragraph for a new speaker

— comma at the end, inside quotation mark

— new speaker, and new paragraph

"You're late for the third time," said MON-I. "You have a half-hour detention tonight." — exact words need quotation marks

You will need this information to do the next bridge activity.

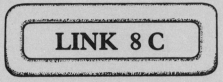

LINK 8 C

The cartoon in Link 8 A shows you a world of science fiction. This dictation passage comes from Monica Hughes's science fiction novel, *The Tomorrow City*. In this novel, C-Three, a computer, is working to create a city that is perfect for children to grow up in. But some strange things happen. As this dialogue points out, too much control can be a bad thing.

This conversation occurs between Caroline, or Caro for short, and her friend David. Be certain to
a) start a new paragraph for each speaker.
b) place quotation marks around the words of each speaker.

> David said, "C-Three has really taken care of everything."
> Caro answered, "But we can't be completely cut off! We'd have read about it in the papers." She stopped at the expression in David's face.
> David said, "All the news that C-Three thinks fit to print."

adapted from Monica Hughes, *The Tomorrow City*

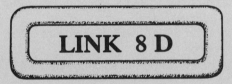

LINK 8 D

Here are some things to do with **quotation marks:**

1. Make up a short dialogue, like the story of Pavlo and MON-I, using one of these situations:
   a) a computer and a dog
   b) two friends
   c) a seagull and a duck
   d) a running shoe and a ballet slipper

2. Listen to two people talking, for about three or four minutes. Be sure to get their permission first. Write their conversation in your notebook.

3. Listen to a three- or four-minute segment of a TV program. It would be helpful if you can audiotape it. Copy this dialogue in your notebook.

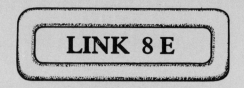

LINK 8 E

1. Listen as your teacher reads the following sentences. Each sentence describes a scene.

2. In your notebook or on separate sheets of paper, sketch the scene that each sentence suggests.

3. Exchange your drawings in small groups. Check to see how many details each person remembered and included in his or her sketch.

4. Look at your drawing. In your notebook write another sentence to describe the scene.

Sentences:

a) We saw the smooth, gray form of the warship glide under the suspension bridge, making smooth ripples in the harbour.

b) City Hall in Toronto stands tall, like a soldier at attention, guarding the little water fountain in the courtyard.

c) Three stately portraits hung from the oak wall of the board room, staring down at the marble-topped table.

d) Mcleod Trail twists through Calgary, a gray line snaking among silent houses.

e) Stanley Park guards the entrance to Vancouver Harbour, tall pines and gray rock looking across a swirling ocean.

f) The fog crept over St. John's harbour, covering the ships along the pier, the moon half-hidden by clouds.

g) The canoe slipped silently through the cold water, passed rocky hills and green pines, on its way to Northern Ontario.

h) The Frontenac Hotel stands firmly on top of a high cliff, overlooking the small houses and shops in Lower Quebec City.

i) The hills of Riding Mountain National Park stood solid and black in the distance, like a fortress rising from the flat plains of Manitoba.

j) The foreboding iceberg stood firm on the quiet seas, a massive triangle of white ice, dwarfing the seagulls that glided slowly in the clear sky.

Which sentences do each of these drawings illustrate? Has the artist included all of the detail suggested in the sentences?

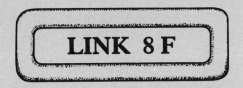

LINK 8 F

The next chapter will introduce you to report writing. One important skill in report writing is the ability to ask questions. This activity gives you practice in asking good questions.

1. One student in the class goes to the front of the classroom and makes a statement.
   Examples:
   I have just seen a good movie.
   I believe that the mayor should impose a nine o'clock curfew on all teenagers.
   Thereafter, this student cannot make any more statements. Rather, he or she can only answer questions.

2. Class members must ask questions of the student who has made the statement. They should find out as much as possible about the student's thinking on his or her subject.
   Examples:
   What movie did you see?
   Who were the stars?
   What was it about?
   Was it similar to any of the stories that we read in literature class?
   Why did you like it?

3. Repeat this exercise several times, using different students and different topics.

   Discussion: When the class has repeated this task several times, discuss this question: *What makes a good question?*

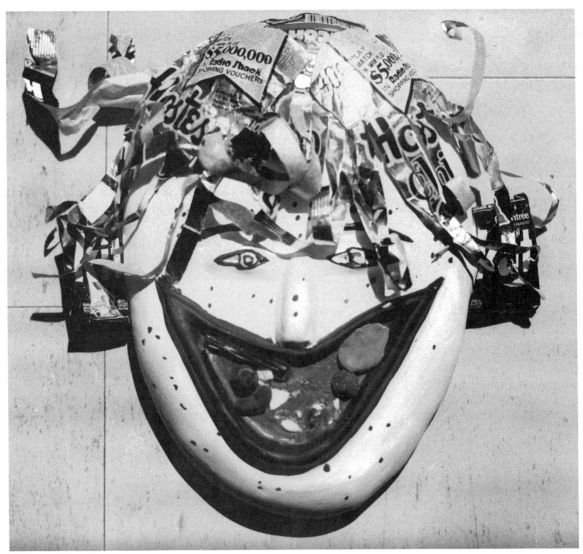

God of Junk Food, Gurdawar Sihra

CHAPTER 8

FLAVIA TELLS ALL—

In school, you are often asked to write reports. Science teachers, social studies teachers, home economics teachers — all kinds of teachers will ask you to write about some topic in their subject area. Unless you know how to go about doing this writing task, reports can be a big headache.

This chapter is about report writing. It will give you a system for preparing a subject-area report. It will help you decide what to write about and how to write it. You will be able to use this system for reports in all of your subjects.

Activity 8A   Report Topics

Write a report of about five pages on one of these topics:

1. what teenagers think about war

2. the place of amateur sport in society

3. television today

4. politics

5. computers in our society

6. city life and country life

7. a famous person from Canada's past

8. a modern-day Canadian hero or heroine

9. your own topic, approved by your teacher

STOP THE PRESS!

This task is too hard to do without some special help. Flavia comes to your rescue. She'll give you some good advice that will help you do Activity 8A.

FLAVIA TELLS ALL
WRITING a REPORT

HI, I'M FLAVIA. I WAS IN GRADE SEVEN LAST YEAR SO I CAN GIVE YOU SOME ADVICE.

... LIKE YOU, MY TEACHER GAVE ME REPORTS TO WRITE.

CLASS, YOUR ASSIGNMENT IS...

THEY TOOK ME SO MUCH TIME — I GUESS I DIDN'T REALLY KNOW *HOW* TO WRITE THEM!

IT WAS HARD TO FIND BOOKS TO FIT THE TOPIC

AND MY REPORTS WERE ALWAYS SO *LONG*.

HEY — I DIDN'T KNOW THAT!

BUT WITH THE HELP OF SOME OF MY TEACHERS, I'VE FOUND A WAY THAT HELPS ME WITH REPORT WRITING...

...AND ON TIME, TOO!

134

NOW I'D LIKE TO SHARE MY METHOD WITH **YOU** —

FIRST, YOUR TEACHER GIVES YOU A TOPIC. WELL, USUALLY IT'S A LIST OF TOPICS...

... AND YOU HAVE TO CHOOSE ONE.

TOPICS:

TEACHERS ARE GOOD AT FINDING HARD TOPICS!

ENCYCLOPEDIA VOL. 4723

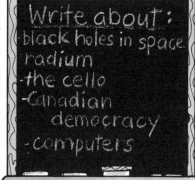

Write about:
- black holes in space
- radium
- the cello
- Canadian democracy
- computers

IF YOU HAVEN'T HAD TOPICS LIKE THESE, JUST WAIT...

THEY'RE COMING!!

CONTINUED...

135

I'VE WRITTEN REPORTS — BIG ONES, LITTLE ONES — ON ALL THESE TOPICS — AND OTHERS BESIDES.

THE BIG QUESTION IS: WHAT TO **DO** ABOUT ALL OF THIS?

HI, KID!

IF YOU'RE LUCKY, YOU'LL HAVE A BRAINY OLDER SISTER OR BROTHER...

... WHO JUST **LOVES** TO DO REPORTS AND WILL ASK TO WRITE YOURS!

MORE PAPER, PLEASE.

SCRIBBLE SCRIBBLE

BUT — IF YOU'RE LIKE ME...

POOF!

... YOU JUST HAVE TO FIND YOUR OWN WAY.

SO — HERE'S **MY** SYSTEM!

The first step is to get to know your topic. Most kids get a book to read, like an encyclopedia, and copy it to write their reports. They change the sentences just a little, but use all of the ideas from the source book. I've discovered that my essays are dull if I do it this way. I learned how to work at my topic, to think about it, and to write notes to myself first. This way I get a report which is my very own thoughts and my own words.

Let's work through the science report that I did last week: *Our Environment*. Here's how I went about doing it.

Step One: Get to Know Your Topic

I picked up my journal writing book and wrote to myself. I started with the word *environment* and wrote to myself for fifteen minutes. I didn't worry about anything other than getting my ideas on the page. Sentences, paragraphs, spelling, commas—none of these things is important here. I also used this writing to meet my journal assignment. Smart, aren't I?

Here is one section of notes. I've recopied them so you can read them.

> **Notes**
>
> I think pollution is ruining our land. I wonder what will become of our animals because of the pollution. Hunters could kill out all the animals. People are polluting our world. We need to find new places to put waste so as not to pollute. We should use our mining resources wisely. When they strip mine they should plant trees in the empty space. I wonder what will happen to our soil. I wonder if we are using our soil resources wisely. Our water is being polluted. The fish are going to die out because of water pollution. We should make sure we are not using up all our fish and if so do something about it. We get lumber from trees. Acid rain is ruining our soil. We get lots of food and jobs from farming. Nature is beautiful. The sun gives us energy....

Now I had a starting point. I knew what I thought about our environment. And I also had my own words or language in my journal. I could use these words later in writing my report. I didn't have to borrow words from a book. Now that I knew what *I* knew about our environment and society, I was ready to find more information.

Step Two: Brainstorm About Your Topic

Our teacher, Mr. Davidsmeier, also helped our class to think about this big topic, the environment. He had us do a thought web. Here is mine:

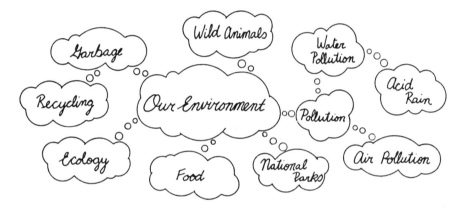

Next Mr. Davidsmeier had our class brainstorm a list of words connected with *our environment*. Here are some of the words our class thought of.

air   sun   acid rain
mining   lakes   smog
cars   oceans   pipelines
packaging   fish   power
                         atmosphere

Then we had to copy these words into our notebooks in complete sentences, like this:

> 1. Our air is getting more polluted each year.
> 2. We are running out of fossil fuels.
> 3. Strip mining ruins the land.
> 4. Packaging for foods consumes a lot of natural resources.

Mr. Davidsmeier calls this whole activity **word finding.**

Step Three: Discuss Your Topic With Others

I should have talked this topic over with my writing group. But I didn't do this step. Mr. Davidsmeier was in a hurry to get through our science unit before spring break. He didn't have time to let us talk about our topic in class. This would have been useful. Maybe I missed a brilliant idea by not asking my friend Tanya about her thoughts on this topic.

Step Four: Conduct Interviews

Instead, I went out and interviewed four people. I asked them what they thought about *our environment.* Here is the list of questions I made up:

> *Flavia's Interview Questions*
> 1. What do you think is one of the worst things happening in our environment?
> 2. What are a few of the things that cause pollution?
> 3. What are some things people could do to help stop pollution?
> 4. Do you think the pipeline being built from Alaska to the U.S.A. is good or bad? Why?
> 5. Do you think people are using our fossil fuels wisely?
> 6. What could people do to help use our fossil fuels more wisely?

7. What do you think we will do when our fossil fuels are gone? What will we replace them with?
8. Do you think the rivers and lakes are being polluted so much that the fish will die out?
9. Do you think the chemicals added to foods to preserve them are healthy?
10. Do you think we are running our wildlife and if so why?

FLAVIA in CONDUCTING an INTERVIEW

PSSST— I'VE INCLUDED A COPY OF THE NOTES THAT OUR TEACHER GAVE US ABOUT CONDUCTING AN INTERVIEW...

...SO ELDON AND I DID A PRACTICE INTERVIEW.

YES, I WAS THE WINNER OF A SCHENLEY AWARD FOR THE MOST OUTSTANDING CANADIAN ROOKIE IN THE CFL...

FLAVIA!!?! YAY! HURRA

FAT CHANCE THAT I'D EVER WIN THIS AWARD...

BUT IT WAS FUN!!

140

NOTES ON CONDUCTING AN INTERVIEW

Interviewing is not as easy as it seems. Use these notes to prepare for your interviews.

1. Plan carefully before you go to an interview.
   - Know the main questions that you want to ask.
   - Write some of these questions out ahead of time.

2. Phone ahead to make arrangements.
   - Remember you are asking someone to give you something. Be polite and pleasant.
   - Try not to make the time inconvenient for your subject.
   - If you have to change the time, be sure to let your subject know. Phone as soon as you can.

3. Practise making your first contact and asking your questions.
   - Use one or two of your friends as guinea pigs. Try out your plans on them.

4. Be aware of the time involved in your interview.
   - Don't be late.
   - Know when you should stop the interview, and stick to your deadline as closely as possible. You should make your interview 20 minutes long, and rarely more than 30 minutes.

5. Plan ahead to take notes.
   - If you can write fast, you might be able to take good notes while you are talking.
   - You might think about asking a friend to take notes for you.
   - If your subject doesn't mind, use a tape recorder and play it back later. Then take notes from the tape. (Some people don't like tape recorders. Be sure to ask first. Most people will forget about the tape after a few minutes. If your subject really objects, don't use the tape.)

6. Think about the interview situation carefully.
   - Arrange the seating so that you and your subject are facing each other. (Watch how a talk show on TV is arranged.)
   - Be sure that you and your subject can make eye contact. If you are going to talk with someone, you have to be able to look at him or her.

7. Use your plans wisely.
   - Keep your plans in front of you and use them to make sure that you ask all of your questions.

- Be flexible if necessary. Your subject may tell you something that you hadn't thought of. Pick up this lead. But know how to get back to the questions you want to ask.

8. Be sure to thank your subject when you finish the interview.
   - You might do something special for your subject, like go visit your subject, or write a short bread and butter letter.
   - You might give your subject a copy of your finished report.

Step Five: Summarize Your Interview Findings

Now it was necessary to make sense out of my interview notes. I reread them and listened to my tapes. I tried to group the answers, to find out exactly what I was interested in. I wrote a summary of my interviews in my notebook, using the heading *Interview Findings*. This writing was just notes, so I didn't pay much attention to mechanics and sentences and spelling. I kept my mind on my ideas.

Here is some of what I wrote:

- While the foods itself may be pure and goods for you, it is often served under unhealthy, unsanitary conditions. ex. fresh vegetables sprayed with dangerous bug-killing sprays, apples, bananas and oranges dyed to make them look brighter, antibiotics put in to animals to keep them free of disease later to end up in our meat
- artificial colours and flavours are no good for you ex. red maraschino cherries are considered by nutritionists as one of the worst foods for this.
- not all foods checked by the F.D.A. are safe, a bleach called agene was used for 30 years before its harm to humans was discovered

- according to F.D.A. rules an 245 grams serving of chocolate can be sold if it contains less than 150 insect fragments and four rodent hairs, peanut butter has a limit of 50 insect fragments for 100 grams. tomato juice has a limit of 10 fruit larvae in 100 grams.

Step Six: Create Questions About Your Subject

After I finished my journal writing and my interview notes, I had some idea of what this report should be like. So I put my journal and interview notes in front of me and made up some questions about my subject.

Questions about my Subject
1. What is the main cause of pollution?
2. If the chemicals being added to food are not healthy why do we add them?
3. Should these chemicals be added to preserve food?
4. Should these chemicals be tested more before being added to foods?
5. What could we do to help our wildlife have a future?
★6. Are the chemicals being added to food good or bad?

I placed a ★ beside question 6. This was obviously the topic that interested me most.

Step Seven: Read About Your Subject

Next I decided to read about what some other people had said about my topic. I asked our librarian, Mrs. Ching, to help me find more information. She was very helpful. She showed me how to look up the subject in the card catalogue. I found three books and chose *Bugs in the Peanut Butter* because I could read it quite easily. Then I shut my book and wrote some points from *Bugs* in my notebook. I made sure that I mentioned that these ideas came from this book. Be sure to write down a complete reference for your books — author, title, publisher, and date of publication. You will need this information for your final copy.

Here is my list of references. They are listed alphabetically by the last name of the author. This list is also called a **bibliography.**

References

Gilbert, Sara. *You Are What You Eat.* Macmillan Publishing Co., Inc., 1977.

Korhanen, Matti. *Seeds — 6.* Science Research Associates, 1981.

Weiner, Michael A. *Bugs in the Peanut Butter.* Little, Brown and Company (Canada) Limited, 1976.

Step Eight: Narrow Your Topic

Next, I looked over my journal, my interview notes, my resource notes, and my questions. Then I made a decision about what my report was about — what I really wanted to say about our environment.

Here is the one big question that I thought my report should answer:

What happens to food in our society?

Step Nine: Discuss Your Topic Again

I was lucky for this step. My mother was home with a sprained ankle, so she had a lot of time to talk with me. I told her about my ideas and discussed them with her. It was good to get a chance to say my ideas out loud.

If you don't have a mother with a sprained ankle handy, you could talk with anyone who will listen. What are best friends for? If you are really lucky, your teacher will give you time to do this kind of discussion in class.

Step Ten: Write Your Thought Draft

Next, I had a spare period in school, so I went to our library and took a table all by myself. I sat down and wrote out my report, as fast as I could—without worrying about sentence structure, commas, spelling, and all those sorts of things. It took me about twenty-five minutes to do this. Mr. Davidsmeier calls this our **thought draft.** In this draft, I found out exactly what my report was about.

Step Eleven: Write an Outline

Now I really had some idea about my subject: problems with food. I wanted to answer this main question: "What are some of the problems in the preparation of food in our society?" When I looked at my thought draft, I noted that I wanted to talk about what happens to our food. So, I made the following outline. It is not a great outline, nothing like the ones you find in textbooks. But it worked for me.

Outline for Essay on Food in our Environment	
1. Definition	4. Junk Food
2. The contents of our food	5. Packaging
3. Nutrition	6. Conclusion

Step Twelve: Use Charts and Illustrations

Mr. Davidsmeier told us that we should include charts and illustrations in our report. These add interest. They also help emphasize the important points, making it easier for readers to remember what you are saying.

I didn't include a very good chart in my report. Instead, I'll show you one from my friend's report.

This is Jenni's drawing of the food chain:

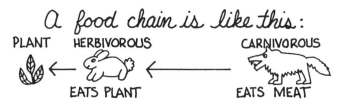

By the way, you should put your charts and drawing on separate pages. This way you don't have to rewrite them from one draft to the next.

Step Thirteen: Write and Revise Your First Draft

The thinking part of this report was now over. The rest was easy. Well, maybe not easy, but I knew exactly what to do.

Using my outline, I worked out a **first draft** of my report. At this point, Mr. Davidsmeier gave us some time in class to work on our reports. We went into our writing groups. I had two of my friends read my report. They pointed out what they thought was good about what I had written. And they gave me a couple of ideas to add to my report. Sue suggested that I drop a couple of points out of the negative part of the report because they really weren't very strong arguments.

Step Fourteen: Prepare Your Final Copy

Next, I was ready to do my **final copy.** I stayed after school on Friday, would you believe it, and by 4:45 I had finished it. I made sure that I added a title page, and also attached my list of references.

Here is the order for the report:

1. title page

2. table of contents

3. body of the report

4. list of references or bibliography

Step Fifteen: Proofread Your Final Copy

On Monday, Mr. Davidsmeier gave us some writing time again. Our writing group used this time to proofread each other's writing. We looked for problems with spelling and punctuation. Because our writing group is quite good at this kind of thing, I didn't have too many problems.

FLAVIA'S WAY

SO, THIS IS THE SYSTEM I WORKED OUT TO HELP ME WRITE REPORTS.

I NOW USE IT FOR ALMOST ALL THE REPORTS I HAVE TO DO.

I DON'T USE ALL THE STEPS EVERY TIME— BUT I FIND I USE MOST OF THEM.

STEPS IN WRITING A REPORT:
1. GET TO KNOW YOUR TOPIC.
2. BRAINSTORM ABOUT YOUR TOPIC.
3. DISCUSS YOUR TOPIC WITH OTHERS.
4. CONDUCT INTERVIEWS.
5. SUMMARIZE FINDINGS.
6. CREATE QUESTIONS.
7. READ ABOUT YOUR TOPIC.
8. NARROW
9. DISC   PIC
10. T   AFT

YOU KNOW— IT REALLY HELPS TO **TALK** TO PEOPLE WHO KNOW ABOUT YOUR TOPIC— BEFORE YOU START A REPORT.

THIS HELPS YOU LEARN **ABOUT** YOUR TOPIC...

CELLULAR
RELATIVITY
RADIATION
ANTIDISESTABLISHMENTARIANISM
VITRIFY
ANTHRO MORPHIC
STIMULUS
RESONATE

AND WHEN YOU *KNOW YOUR TOPIC*— IT CAN EVEN BE **FUN** TO WRITE A REPORT!

by Flavia

Steps in Writing a Report: A Summary

1. Get to Know Your Topic

2. Brainstorm About Your Topic

3. Discuss Your Topic With Others

4. Conduct Interviews

5. Summarize Your Interview Findings

6. Create Questions About Your Subject

7. Read About Your Subject

8. Narrow Your Topic

9. Discuss Your Topic Again

10. Write Your Thought Draft

11. Write an Outline

12. Use Charts and Illustrations

13. Write and Revise Your First Draft

14. Prepare Your Final Copy

15. Proofread Your Final Copy

LINK 9 A

1. Look at this cartoon.

2. Create your own cartoon to show these phrases:
   a) red in the face
   b) caught red-handed
   c) feather-brained
   d) hard-nosed
   e) your own word or phrase

"You have 'guilty' written all over your face."

LINK 9 B

In the last chapter on report writing, you discovered that it is often necessary to make up questions to write a report. If you ask good questions, you will probably be able to find good answers.

This activity gives you more practice in making up good questions:

1. You are the host or hostess of a fast-paced interview program on radio. The program is broadcast on weekdays, right after school.

2. You have to keep the action moving to keep the interest of your teenaged audience. For this reason, you are able to ask your guests only three questions — so they have to be the best three questions possible.

3. In your notebook, write the three questions you would ask each of these people:
   a) a sixteen-year-old student who has just won $1 000 000 in a provincial lottery
   b) a twelve-year-old patient who has just won a battle with cancer or some other disease

c) a person who has just celebrated an eightieth birthday
d) a talking pig
e) a teenager who has just won a scholarship to a prestigious ballet school in Toronto
f) a goalie who lost three teeth during a hockey game
g) a subject of your choice

Extension: In small groups of three or four students, use a cassette recorder to role-play this radio interview program.

Be sure to interview all of the people from the above list. Share your questions so that you can choose the best three questions for each situation.

Add music and other topics of interest to your tape, but it should not exceed twelve minutes in length.

Play your tape in another classroom and ask the class to rate your program.

1	2	3	4	5	6
so-so		ho-hum			a hit

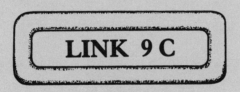

LINK 9 C

This paragraph is written following this model:

main idea + supporting details

Jogging Shoes

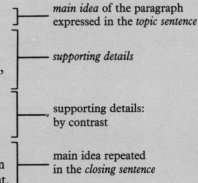

Proper jogging shoes serve several important functions. These include protecting the foot from running surfaces, supporting the foot structure, cushioning, giving traction, and balancing foot deformation. Poor quality or improperly fitting shoes can lead to everything from blisters to achilles tendinitis. A good and proper fitting pair of shoes is without question the jogger's most important investment.

main idea of the paragraph expressed in the *topic sentence*

supporting details

supporting details: by contrast

main idea repeated in the *closing sentence*

1. Read this list of features for proper jogging shoes:

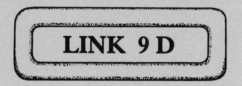

   a) a good fit
   b) a firm and rigid heel counter
   c) ample toe room
   d) lateral (sideways) stability
   e) a flexible sole
   f) a firm arch support
   g) adequate cushioning from heel to toe

2. Combine these details into one paragraph using this model: main idea expressed in a topic sentence + supporting details.

LINK 9 D

An important skill in writing is being able to organize information. The outline helps you do this. It helps you see **main ideas** and **supporting details.**

This outline contains three main ideas, with supporting details.

1. Copy the outline into your notebook.

2. Fill in this outline with the right title, main ideas, and supporting details:

_____
   (title)

1.
   A.
   B.
   C.
   D.

2.
   A.
   B.

3.
   A.
   B.

apple pie
candy
Coca-Cola®
drinks
cake
7-Up®
sweet things
dessert
ice cream
pudding
chocolate
lollipops

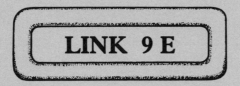

LINK 9 E

This dictation passage comes from a short story, ''Grandfather's Special Magic.'' Little Cloud leaves the city every summer to spend time with his grandfather in the Muskoka region of Ontario. Little Cloud's grandfather has a special magic: a way with animals.

As he ran from the cabin into the early morning sunlight, the slight, copper-coloured boy could see his grandfather in the paddock working with the new pony. Calling and waving his hand, the boy ran to the fence and climbed onto the top rail.

The sudden movement startled the chestnut horse and she reared, thrashing her hooves and straining to be free of the rope looped around her neck. Her thick, golden mane flew as her head tossed angrily from side to side.

Elizabeth Kaufman, ''Grandfather's Special Magic''

Extension: Rewrite this dictation passage in your notebook, following these directions:

1. Change the verbs from the past tense form to the present tense form.

2. Cut out all adjectives (but not pronoun adjectives like *his* and *hers*).

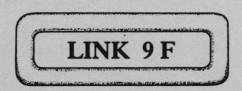

LINK 9 F

This activity is about **listening** for the **main idea** and **supporting details.**

1. Listen as your teacher reads each of these paragraphs. Decide on the main idea for each paragraph and the supporting details that connect with the main idea.

2. One supporting detail does not belong in each paragraph. It does not connect to the main idea.

3. Write this **unconnected** sentence in your notebook.

a) One day the black dog walked down the street. She held her head and tail high. She had finally won her freedom, after three year's trying. The calico cat jumped onto the horse's back. The gate had been left open, and she was proudly on her way to visit that smart aleck poodle who lived at the end of the block.

b) Last summer we got an orange-coloured kitten. We called him Chester, after much debate and consideration. Our house hasn't been the same since. My mother fed the old cat some catnip. He climbs curtains, terrorizes the dog, and walks all over the table. The name Chester rather suits him, as in chest*nut*.

Extension: Try your hand at a listening exercise. Find a paragraph that you have written, perhaps in your writing folder or in your journal. Rewrite it, and insert one detail that does not connect with the main idea. Read your paragraph in small groups. Have your small group members identify the **unconnected** sentence.

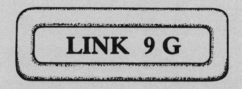

Here is a telephone conversation between Hilary and Leslie, two grade seven students. You are given only Hilary's speech.

1. In pairs, read this dialogue. One student reads Hilary's part, and the other makes up Leslie's part in the conversation.

2. Reverse roles and make up a new dialogue.

3. Form small groups. Each pair will repeat one of its dialogues. This time the student who reads Leslie's part will give one statement that is totally unconnected to Hilary's statement. Members of the small group will listen to identify the **unconnected** statement in the dialogue.

Discussion: Did the dialogue make sense, and follow in logical order? Did the pair use the right intonation in their voices? That is, did the conversation sound right? In what different ways did the readers say the little words and phrases like "Oh!" and "I'll see you then"? How did each person say, "Hello, Leslie"?

Script

Hilary: Hello, Leslie.

Leslie: _____

Hilary: Did you get the answer to the second math question?

Leslie: _____

Hilary: Oh!

Leslie: _____

Hilary: I don't see it that way.

Leslie: _____

Hilary: That makes sense to me. I'll try to keep your advice in mind.

Leslie: _____

Hilary: Leslie, you always have a simple solution for everything.

Leslie: _____

Hilary: I'd like to. When should we meet?

Leslie: _____

Hilary: OK. I'll see you then.

Leslie: _____

PEANUTS featuring "Good ol' Charlie Brown" by Schulz

New Hamster ✓
Coral See ✓
Daffnee & Kloey ✓
1614 ✓
1902 ✓
Gregory XCM ✓
See Odder ✓

YES, MA'AM, I GOT ALL FIFTY QUESTIONS WRONG...

I DON'T THINK IT WAS MY FAULT, THOUGH..

1-24

LAST NIGHT I WAS WATCHING A PROGRAM ON TV THAT I DIDN'T WANT TO MISS...THEN I HAD TO READ THE SPORTS SECTION IN THE PAPER...

THERE'S ALSO THIS TALK SHOW ON THE RADIO THAT I LISTEN TO EVERY NIGHT...

© 1982 United Feature Syndicate, Inc.

AND TWO OF MY MAGAZINES CAME IN THE MAIL YESTERDAY..

I BLAME IT ON THE MEDIA!

CHAPTER 9

SOMETHING FOR EVERYBODY: LET'S LOOK AT MAGAZINES

Many of the choices you make each day have to do with the **mass media.** Television, radio, movies, newspapers, and magazines all compete for your time. Each one wants to win your attention. There are only so many hours in a day, though. You must know how to use the mass media so you can choose your entertainment wisely and gain the information you want quickly.

In other words, you need to be able to **analyze** sources of entertainment and information. This chapter will help you practise some skills of analysis as you look at one of the mass media: **magazines**.

MAGAZINES IN YOUR LIFE

Beware!

They lurk in the aisles of your favourite cornerstore and live in the quiet, clean medicine smell of your favourite drug store. They hang around newsstands, libraries, and bookstores and even invade your home through the mail. They're out to get your attention and will do all kinds of things to catch your eye. They're part of a multi-million dollar industry which grows larger each year. They're magazines, of course, and they come in all shapes and sizes.

Activity 9A   Look at Me: I'm Great

1. Look at the magazine covers.
   a) Why do most magazine publishers use pictures on the front cover?
   b) How do magazine covers use words to appeal to your curiosity?

2. As a class, talk about how magazines try to attract your attention.

Just as various movies and television programs compete for your attention, thousands of magazine titles also try to get your attention. Have magazines invaded your life?

Activity 9B   What's in a Title?

1. Form a group of three or four students and brainstorm the following questions, making sure a group recorder writes down your ideas:
   a) List all the magazine titles you can think of.
   b) Which of these magazines have you read?
   c) What are your favourite magazines?
   d) Why do people read magazines?

2. Have someone in your group report to the class, using a chart:
   a) How many magazine titles did the group think of?
   b) What are the favourite magazines of group members?
   c) How many reasons for reading magazines did the group think of? What are they?

Something for Everybody

Do magazines have something for everybody? Media watchers have discovered there are over 50 000 English-language magazine titles in circulation. Fifty of these titles have a circulation of over a million or more! Which is the one with the largest circulation? You guessed it — *T. V. Guide!* One mass medium supports another! And it's all based on something everyone must learn to do — to use language with a specific purpose and to connect with various audiences.

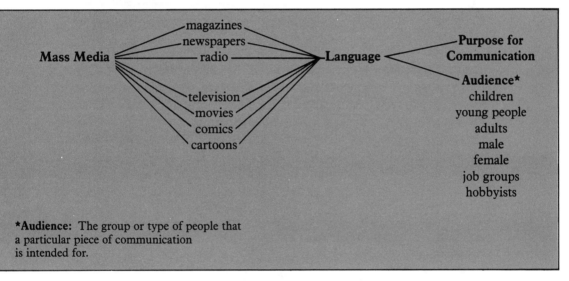

Mass Media — magazines, newspapers, radio, television, movies, comics, cartoons — **Language** — **Purpose for Communication**, **Audience***: children, young people, adults, male, female, job groups, hobbyists

*Audience: The group or type of people that a particular piece of communication is intended for.

Magazines, like all mass media, use language for specific purposes aimed at specific audiences.

Activity 9C   Canadian Content

1. Look at a copy of any Canadian magazine. (You should be able to find one at home or in your school library.)

2. What is the general subject of the magazine? It could be such topics as current affairs, decorating, fishing, travelling, cooking, dance, or science fiction.

3. Who will likely read this magazine?

4. How does the magazine communicate its information: by words? by photographs? by graphs or charts? other?

Magazines are a major factor in the world's mass communication. Have a closer look at magazines as you learn about and practise some of the skills of **analysis.**

PLAYING DETECTIVE

Writing an Analysis

When you write an analysis, you play detective. You begin with a question or series of questions about something or the way something works. You then gather information and use the information to answer your question(s).

Analysis helps you solve problems you wish to investigate. Analysis begins with curiosity and ends with the sharing of information.

How should you approach an analysis? As any detective approaches a case, of course. Systematically! Here are some guidelines to help you complete an analysis in an organized manner:

a) **State clearly what it is you want to find out.**
   • A clear purpose and direction is a must.

b) **Form a plan to collect information.**
   • Analysis is based on **data:** facts and the relationships among facts that you discover.

c) **Use the plan to gather information.**
   • Observe. Read. Survey. Talk to people, listen to music . . . do what you must to gather your information.

d) **Draw conclusions from your information.**
   • Study your information in order to decide what it means.

A Sample Analysis

You can see how an analysis develops by looking at the example. Here's what one student did to find out if advertising had any influence on teenagers' choice of fast-food restaurants.

Read this analysis and notice how it is organized. The writer is careful to work through each of the steps in the system:

- What I wanted to find out (**questions**)
- What I did (**a plan to gather information**)
- What I observed (**the information gathered**)
- What I concluded (**the meaning of the information**)

A Sample Analysis

Does Advertising Count? Teens' Choices of Eating Places

What I Wanted to Find Out:
Fast-food restaurants are very popular among teens today. Each one offers the same kinds of food — hamburgers, french fries, milkshakes, and soft drinks — but each one tries to be a little different. These restaurants spend a lot of money on advertising. Chirpy's, McBerry's, and Sally's, in particular, spend millions of dollars as they compete with each other. Does this advertising make any difference? How much attention do teens give to these ads and do the ads influence them?

What I Did:
I surveyed 50 seventh-grade students at St. Laurent School to ask them to state their favourite fast-food restaurant ad. The ad could be from television, radio, magazine, billboard, or newspaper. I then asked the students if the ad had made them select that restaurant as their favourite fast-food place. If the answer to the second question was "no," I asked the students why they preferred a different restaurant.

What I Observed:
Most students (37 out of 50) chose the McBerry's ad, with the clown and the talking french fries as their

favourite. Six persons chose the Chirpy's ad with the magician, and the other seven chose the Sally's ad with the girls' football team. All ads chosen were from television. When I asked them if the ad made them select that restaurant as their favourite, 40 out of the 50 students said "yes." They chose as their favourite fast-food restaurant the one they named in their favourite ad. They said the ad makes the restaurant look great, so they go there. The other ten said that although they like the ad of one, the food was tastier for them at the other restaurant.

What I Concluded:
Most of the students seem to be influenced by fast-food restaurant advertising. They admit that they go to restaurants because of the advertising. It is reasonable to conclude that as far as grade 7 students at St. Laurent are concerned, these restaurants — especially McBerry's — are spending their advertising money wisely. Teens are paying attention to these ads and are influenced by them.

Activity 9D   An Analysis of an Analysis

1. In groups of three or four, take a good look at this sample analysis of teens' choices of eating places.

2. Appoint a group recorder for discussion and use the following questions to guide your discussion:
   a) How is the analysis organized?
   b) What are the questions the writer sets out to answer?
   c) If you were conducting this analysis, what would you have done differently?
   d) Why does the writer include precise results in the observations (i.e., 37 out of 50 students . . . 40 out of 50 students)?
   e) Is the conclusion acceptable? Why or why not?

3. Using your recorded ideas as a starting point, list at least *five* things found in a good analysis.

4. Copy these points into your notebook to help you when you are writing an analysis.

Getting Started

It's time for you to use these guidelines to do an analysis. Later in the chapter you will be doing an analysis concerned with magazines available for Canadian teenagers.

Activity 9E   Three Situations for You to Solve

1. Working alone or with a partner, write in your notebook a plan for carrying out an analysis of the three situations that follow. In each case:
   a) You are given a question or problem.
   b) Follow the outline as it is given.
   c) For parts C and D of each analysis, predict what you *might* observe and what a probable conclusion might be.

Remember: To predict an answer, you do not actually complete the analysis. Your conclusion will be a guess only, since you haven't carried out your research.

Situation 1

1. What I want to find out:
   How many students in the class read sports magazines? What is the most popular sports magazine they read?

2. What I might do to find out:

3. What I might observe:

4. What I might conclude:

Situation 2

1. What I want to find out:
   Do grade 7 students spend more time on a regular basis reading newspapers or magazines?

2. What I might do to find out:

3. What I might observe:

4. What I might conclude:

Situation 3

1. **What I want to find out:**
   What are the most popular magazines among grade 7 students at my school?

2. **What I might do to find out:**

3. **What I might observe:**

4. **What I might conclude:**

2. As a class, listen as several class members read their plans for their analyses.
   a) Be prepared to comment on whether or not each plan could be improved.
   b) Do you agree with the predicted conclusions? Why or why not? Can you think of reasons why the conclusions might be different?

HERE YOU GO

You've Got a Job To Do!

Let's say you work for a national magazine publisher who puts out several of Canada's widely read magazines. This publisher wants to see how many of these magazines appeal to the Canadian teenager. The company wants to make plans for future publications for young teens and needs information in order to make important decisions. Here's your opportunity for analysis.

You begin this analysis with a prewriting activity: planning and gathering ideas. You already know what you want to find out:

What kinds of magazines are available for Canadian teenagers to read?
You also know *why* you want to find it out:

To help your boss, the magazine publisher, so that he or she can plan future publications for teenagers.

See what you can do.

Activity 9F   Plan Your Work

1. In your notebook, write down a plan for carrying out this analysis.
   a) You must find out what magazines are competing for the attention of Canadian teenagers in your region of Canada.

- Visit your school library, your community library, and other places where you can find magazines.
- List all the titles you can find that appeal to teenagers.
- Add any other titles you are familiar with.

b) Place these titles into categories so you can see the kinds of magazines that are available for teenagers.
- Some categories you might consider are sports magazines, hobby magazines, fiction "mags." Make up any other categories that you need.

2. Gather your information, following through on the plan you have made.

3. In writing teams of two or three people, talk about the information you have gathered.
   a) Remember that everyone's information may be slightly different and may lead to different conclusions. There is no one right answer.
   b) Use the following points to guide your discussion:
      - How many titles could you find for young teens?
      - At what different teen audiences are they aimed?
      - What purposes do they seek to fulfill?
      - Which teen interests seem to have few magazines?
      - In which categories, or kinds of magazines, are there the greatest number of titles?
      - Which magazines do you think attract the widest audience?
      - Which magazines probably have a smaller audience? Why?

4. After you have discussed your information with the writing team, write down your conclusions.
   a) What kind of magazine selection is available for Canadian teens?
   b) Do Canadian teens need more magazines?
   c) What kind of magazine or magazines, if any, should your boss, the publisher, consider producing?

You now have a complete **outline** of your analysis:

- What I wanted to find out
- What I did to find out
- What I observed
- What I concluded

Activity 9G   The Real Thing

1. Follow the stages in the writing process. Use the stages for writing an analysis to help you write a draft copy of your analysis of this problem: What teen magazines could be published in Canada?

2. When you complete your first draft, get together with your writing team once more.
   a) Exchange drafts and read each other's work.
   b) Make any suggestions you can for improvement.
      • Should anything be added? taken out? stated a better way? rearranged?
      • Is the overall organization of the analysis clear, or could it be improved?

3. Make your final copy, doing your editing as you go.

4. Proofread this copy yourself or with the help of someone from your writing team.

Rounding Off

Now you're a little more informed about one important mass medium. Choice is important for effective media use. Learning about analysis can enable you to make better choices. Analysis gives you a fuller understanding of a situation.

Perhaps there are other interesting issues you want to analyze in the way you have learned to do here. Now you know how. Good luck — and happy magazine reading.

LINK 10 A

Ghost Ships B.C. Binning

This painting, *Ghost Ships* by B. C. Binning, hangs in the Art Gallery of Toronto. You can use it to do some more thinking about magazines.

Talk about these questions in class:

1. If you were to see this painting reproduced on the cover of a magazine, what would you expect the magazine to be about? Why?

2. What kind of print would be used for the title on the cover? Why?

3. What colour combinations would be used on the cover:
   a) for the ships and the masts?
   b) for the background?
   c) for the two circles at the top of the painting?

4. Do you like *Ghost Ships*? Why or why not?

5. What is another title for this painting? Why did you choose this title?

LINK 10 B

PLACE NAME CHANT

BELLA BELLA, BELLA COOLA,
ATHABASKA, IROQUOIS:
MESILINKA, OSILINKA,
MISSISSAUGA, MISSISQUOIS.
CHEPPEWA, CHIPPAWA,
NOTTAWASAGA;
OSHAWA, OTTAWA,
NASSAGEWEGA.
MALAGASH, MATCHEDASH,
SHUBENACADIE;
COUCHICHING, NIPPISSING,
SCUBENACADIE.
SHICKSHOCK
YAHK
QUAW!

Meguido Zola

This oral exercise is a *place name chant.*

1. Practise reading this list of Canadian place names on your own.

2. Get a group of about four or five students together. Make an audiotape recording of your reading of this poem. Remember, it is a *chant.*

3. Make up a similar chant of place names in your regions—names of towns, streets, schools, people, and make an audiotape recording of a reading of this poem.

Save your work for a special day in your classroom and impress your visitors!
Extension: How many of these Canadian place names can you locate on a map?

LINK 10 C

Here is an activity to test to see if you can listen carefully enough to remember details:

1. Your teacher will choose three students.
   a) Student A leaves the classroom.
   b) Student B tells the class a short story—something that happened, something overheard, something imagined.
   c) Student C listens to Student B's story.
      Then, Student C goes out of the classroom and tells Student B's story to Student A.
   d) Student A returns to the classroom and retells Student B's story.
   e) Repeat this activity, using different groups of students.

Discussion: After three or four different groups of students have done this activity, talk about the results in class:

1. Does the story lose anything in being retold secondhand? If it does, why, and what does it lose?

2. How well was Student A able to communicate Student B's story? Was anything left out? Was anything added?

3. How do the students who retold the story (Student A's) feel about their task? Was it easy? Did they feel comfortable telling someone's story?

4. What message is there in this activity for the way you should approach your writing assignments?

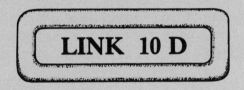

LINK 10 D

This dictation passage comes from a novel called *The Root Cellar* by Janet Lunn. In it, a young girl finds a secret doorway in an old root cellar. The door leads into past time, back to the days in Canada when the Civil War was being fought in the United States. In this passage, Susan and Rose, two young girls, set out to look for Will, who has left Canada to go back to the United States to join the Yankee army and help his relatives in the war.

They did not find Will but they did find Mrs. Fiske's boarding house. Mrs. Fiske herself came to the door, a tall woman with black hair done in a tight knob on the top of her head. Sharp black eyes stared down a long nose at them. Her mouth looked to be permanently pursed in disapproval. She wore a black dress with a white apron over it, and when she talked she jingled the keys that hung from a chain pinned to her apron. They told her they had come to look for their brother Will.

Janet Lunn, *The Root Cellar*

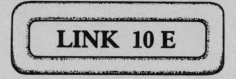

LINK 10 E

This activity will get you thinking about **visual communication** and **visual literacy**, the subject of the next chapter.

"Don't forget to write your name on your paper!" How many times have you heard your teacher give this direction? Artists and people in business don't have to be told to place their signature on their products. Their trademarks are very important to them, and they have been signing their works in unique ways for many centuries.

Here are some *trademarks*, or *logos*, which were used by artisans and merchants several hundred years ago:

The first logo is the watermark of Fabriano, a famous Italian papermaker (1300). The second logo is the engraver's mark of the German artist Albrecht Durer, from the fifteenth century. The third logo is a printer's mark from Brussels, Belgium, in 1476. The fourth logo is an eighteenth-century goldsmith's mark, from France.

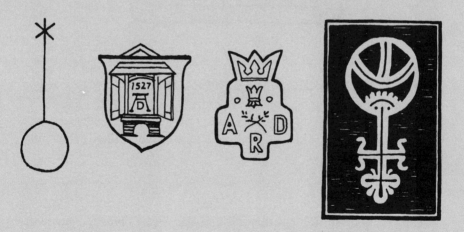

The tradition of placing trademarks on products has developed so that today almost every company has its own logo, which it places on its products.

1. In your notebook, write down the company or association for each of these logos:

Extension: Form a small group. Go searching for logos in magazines and newspapers or advertisements — anywhere you can find them. After getting permission to cut them out, make a display of logos on a large piece of paper. Use this as a class guessing game to see who can identify the most logos. Use the activity in the Link section as a model for your poster display of logos.

Child's Play Bob Iveson and Tom Galli

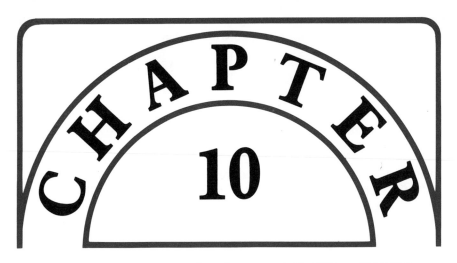

CHAPTER 10

STOP, LOOK — AND SEE

The world is changing. Television made a big impact in the 1950s. In recent years, computers have added to this change. Both television and computers have made **visual communication** possible and easy.

In any one day, you probably receive as much information visually as you do through print. Pictures, signs, logos, advertisements — all of these visual images give you information. You use them and they use you.

This chapter is about **visual communication.** You will find out what this term means and how it works. You will study how colour and shape are used in society to give information and how people react to different types of visual communication.

GETTING STARTED

Unlike other chapters in this text, this one is not about writing. Rather, it's about visual communication — seeing and understanding pictures — as well as about talking. For the work that you do in this special chapter you need a special kind of book to keep it in: a **Visual Literacy Book.**

Activity 10A   A Visual Literacy Book

What kind of special book should you have? Here are some suggestions:

1. a plain folder

2. a duo-tang folder, in your favourite colour

3. a folder you can make yourself from two pieces of cardboard, with some tape to make the spine

4. a box

5. your own idea

Keep your work for this chapter in this folder. At the end of the chapter, you will give your work a proper title, bind it, and illustrate it.

In the meantime it will be called your **Visual Literacy Book.**

To get started, here is a problem to see how well you understand a simple visual message.

Activity 10B   Olympic Symbols

These symbols were used in the 1968 Olympics in Mexico and the 1972 Winter Olympics in Sapporo, Japan. They announced the locations of the events.

1. In your notebook, write the name of the sport suggested by each sign.

2. Talk about these questions in class:
   a) Why is it necessary to use signs to announce the sites of the events?
   b) Do Olympic Games still use these same signs, or have new ones been designed?

From the Olympics in Mexico:

From the Winter Olympics in Sapporo:

THINKING VISUALLY

Let's have a closer look at visual communication. You will examine three basic principles: **colour, shape**, and **line.** The next section will help you learn how colour communicates meaning. The following sections will look at shape and line.

Colour

Activity 10C Colours in Your World

1. **Recopy the following chart in your Visual Literacy Book.**

2. **In the right-hand column, write a short statement to describe what this colour makes you think about or how it makes you feel.**

3. **In a class discussion, compare your answers to those of the other members of your class.**

4. **What conclusions do you reach about the way colours make people feel?**

5. **Include your notes in your Visual Literacy Book.**

The Meaning of Colour	
Colour	*What I think or how I feel*
Red	
Green	
Yellow	
Black	
White	

Does colour convey meaning? The answer is *yes*, for most people. Let's explore this further.

Activity 10D   Colour Me Happy

1. On your own, decide what colour you would use to communicate these feelings:

   sadness

   youthfulness

   happiness

   hatred

   death

   coldness

   life

   warmth

2. Share your reaction to each of these words in a class discussion.

3. Are your colour associations with these words the same as or different from others in your class?

4. What conclusions do you reach as a class about the way different colours make people feel or think?

5. In your Visual Literacy Book, write a set of notes for yourself to summarize your ideas about colour and other people's thoughts and feelings.

By now you will probably agree with this statement: different colours have different meaning attached to them. Most likely your class has agreed on most of the feelings or meaning associated with each colour. Let's use this information about the meaning of colour to convey your personal reaction to a poem.

Activity 10E   The Wind Has Wings

1. Read the following poem. Decide how this poem makes you feel.

2. Select one colour that communicates this feeling.

3. Using a full-sized page in your Visual Literacy Book, create a shape or shapes that communicate your feeling, using the colour you chose.

4. Talk about your results in small groups of three or four people. Use these directions to guide your discussion:
   a) The first group member shows his or her response to the group.
   b) He or she asks the group members to give their interpretation of the shape. That is, they explain how the shape makes them feel or think. Then, the first member tells what he or she intended the drawing to say.
   c) The group repeats this procedure until all members have shown and discussed their responses to "The Wind Has Wings," an Inuit chant.

The Wind Has Wings

Nunaptique . . . In our land — *ahe, ahe, ee, ee, iee*
The wind has wings, winter and summer.
It comes by night and it comes by day,
And children must fear it — *ahe, ahe, ee, ee, iee.*
In our land the nights are long,
And the spirits like to roam in the dark.
I've seen their faces, I've seen their eyes.
They are like ravens, hovering over the dead,
Their dark wings forming long shadows,
And children must fear them — *ahe, ahe, ee, ee, iee.*

Translated by Raymond de Coccola and Paul King

Colours in Combination

Some colour combinations are easier to see than others. Try this experiment to decide which combinations cause shapes to stand out from their background.

Activity 10F   Colours in Contrast

Explore these questions as a whole class.

1. **Look carefully at the following diagrams.**

2. **Decide which colour combinations provide a good contrast, so that the small square stands out easily. Then decide in which combinations the contrast is not so sharp.**

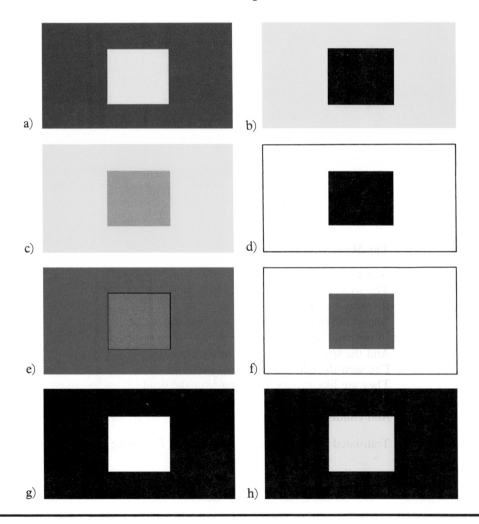

Activity 10G   Royal Purple

Answer the following activity as a whole class.

1. **Look at each diagram intently for thirty seconds.**

2. **Then, answer this question: What happens to the yellow and purple circles in each of these illustrations?**

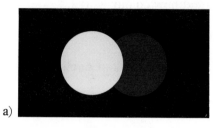 

a)   b)

3. **In the following illustrations, which colour seems closer to you, red or yellow?**

a)   b)

You have seen that different colour combinations provide a different sense of perspective. They can give an illusion of depth, a feeling that something is further back in a picture and that something else is closer. This fact is useful in composing a picture of a visual image that will convey a message. With the right colour combinations, objects stand out in a visual story.

Activity 10H   Magazine Advertisements

1. **Look at the use of colour in the lettering and illustrations in the advertisements of several magazines.**

2. **Cut them out and arrange them as a display in your Visual Literacy Book.**

3. **Use this display to present a short speech to your class to explain how colour is used in advertising.**

Artists, advertising agents, and interior decorators, among others, use colour in their work. They have to know how people react to colour. They use this knowledge to make choices in their work. They also need to know about shape, so let's look now at shapes.

Shapes

Shapes and lines also communicate meaning. It is more difficult to see the way they work than it is to understand how colour works.

Activity 10I And Now . . . Shapes

1. This chart contains some common shapes. Look at each shape for a moment.

2. Complete this chart in your Visual Literacy Book by telling how you feel about the shape and what things or ideas you associate with it.

3. As a class, discuss this question: Of what importance is the fact that shapes have meaning attached to them?

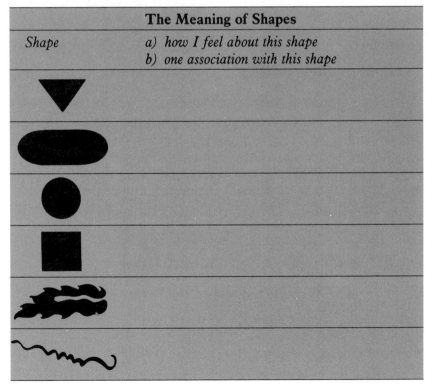

The Meaning of Shapes	
Shape	*a) how I feel about this shape* *b) one association with this shape*

This topic of shapes and their meanings will come up again.

Activity 10J Shapes in Pictures

1. Look at the pictures on this page and on the next page.

2. Write down the letters a to f in your Visual Literacy Book. Beside each, write down a description of the shapes that appear in each photograph.

3. Make a list of those people in your community who are concerned about shapes. Why and how are they concerned?

4. Write notes to yourself about this activity in your Visual Literacy Book.

a)

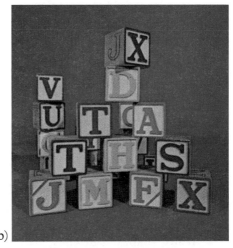

b)

c)

d)

e)

f)

Lines — Special Shapes

Which of these lines is longer?

Measure them to find out. Did you have difficulty arriving at an answer by just looking at the two lines? Why?

Lines play an important role in visual communication. They are really shapes, but they are important enough to be looked at by themselves. A line may be horizontal or vertical, long or short, straight or curved. No matter what its shape, a line can reinforce meaning.

Artists often use lines in paintings to communicate with their viewers. The following reproduction of *Alberta Rhythm*, a Canadian painting, shows how lines work together to produce feeling and meaning. It was painted by A. Y. Jackson, who was one of a group of artists called The Group of Seven.

Activity 10K   Lines: Alberta Rhythm

1. In class, suggest how the lines in this painting provide a feeling of the province of Alberta.

2. Write notes about your discussion in your Visual Literacy Booklet.

Alberta Rhythm by A. Y. Jackson

LOOKING AT PICTURES — VISUAL CLUES

You now know that colour, shape, and line interact to direct or control how you look at a visual image. If you see a shape you like and a colour you like, you have a good feeling about that image. This section will look at other ways to help you understand pictures.

Distance from Subject

Activity 10L   Distance from Subject in Pictures

1. As a whole class, look at these pictures.

2. Which one is a large object taken from a distance, and which one is a small object taken up close?

3. Discuss these questions as a whole class:
   a) What is the effect of the distance of the subject from the camera on the visual impact of a photograph?
   b) How can this information be used in visual communication?

4. Include your notes in your Visual Literacy Book.

The answer to this visual puzzle appears on **page 186.**

Activity 10M   Distance from Subject in Magazine Advertisements

1. Look at the advertisements in several magazines.

2. Select at least six examples of the imaginative use of close-ups, long-shots or perspective, in these ads. Get permission to cut them out.

3. Then arrange your examples to make a display in your Visual Literacy Book.

4. In small groups, explain your display to each other.

5. Choose the best example from your group and one member of your group to explain it to your class.

Activity 10N Distance from Subject on Television

1. Look at advertisements on television, particularly food advertisements or advertisements for toys for little children.

2. Discuss in class how these ads use close-ups, long-shots, or unusual perspective to enhance the image of their products.

3. Write notes to yourself in your Visual Literacy Book. Include examples with your notes. You may have to sketch these examples.

Photographs give you information in other ways. These ways, or visual clues, are such things as lines, blurred images, and the balance of the main image.

Activity 10O Visual Clues in Pictures

1. Examine the pictures on this page.

2. Identify the visual clues for each picture: lines, blurred images, balance of the main image, or distance from the subject.

3. Discuss the information that each clue gives to you.

4. Write your conclusions about visual clues in your Visual Literacy Book.

a)   b)
c)   d)

Activity 10P Visual Clues in Logos

1. Examine the visual clues in the following logos.

2. As a whole class, discuss the ways in which these visual clues work.

3. Think of other logos that are visual clues to reinforce the meaning of the product.

4. Make a display for your Visual Literacy Book.

A picture may contain clues that give you a message. The lines and blurs in pictures suggest motion and give a sense of direction. If a picture is off balance, it also has a sense of motion, seeming to move in the direction in which the image appears to fall.

Activity 10Q Make Your Own Visual Clues

1. Add visual clues to these shapes to give more information about them. The first drawing has been done for you.

2. Next, work in pairs to examine and explain your partner's illustrations.

3. Check to make sure that you and your partner interpret the visual clues in the same way.

4. Include this activity in your Visual Literacy Book.

PUTTING IT ALL TOGETHER

Activity 10R A Shapely Fairy Tale

1. Working alone, think about a common fairy tale or fable.

2. Now, communicate your story visually, using colour, shape, and line, but no words. For example, you might retell the story of *The Three Little Pigs*. You could use different shapes to represent

each of the little pigs, as well as another shape for the wolf. What colour would suggest the nature of each of the little pigs? the big bad wolf?

3. Use comic strip form to present your story, without the talk balloons.

4. When you have finished your story, explain it to a small group of three or four classmates. Have your classmates comment on your visual story so that they can help you be sure that it says what you want it to say.

5. Include this visual story in your Visual Literacy Book.

Activity 10S   Your Visual Literacy Book

In Activity 10A, you began to work on a Visual Literacy Book. Now it's time to do something with all of the material you have collected.

1. Go back over your notes, complete them, and put them in order.

2. Then, decide upon some sections to divide your notes into. You may use the same system outlined in this chapter, or develop your own system.

3. Design title pages for each of these sections. Each page should contain a printed heading to advertise the section, and it should have some kind of visual symbol or image as well.

4. Go over your notes and add headings where necessary.

5. Look at your notes again to decide where you can add more visual images or symbols to help make your notes more attractive and to help communicate the information in your book.

6. Next, create a title for your book. You have been calling it your Visual Literacy Book, but you can probably find a much better title.

7. Finally, design a title page for your book. The title page should have a title as well as a visual image.

Keeping Your Eyes Open

In this chapter, you have been studying **visual literacy.** You have discovered how colour and shape and line have meaning for some people. Some of the activities helped you see how advertising and television use visual communication to get meaning across to viewers.

You saw, too, that the visual clues in a photograph or picture help create meaning: distance from subject, perspective, lines, blurred images, balance of the image. You are beginning to understand how visual communication works.

You now know how *to stop, look — and see.*

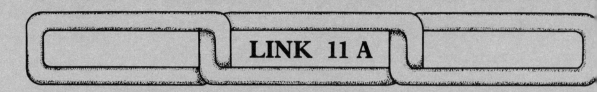

LINK 11 A

This painting by Lawren Harris is titled *Lake Superior*. Mr. Harris, like A. Y. Jackson whose painting we discussed in Chapter 10, was a member of the Group of Seven. Members of this group are among Canada's most famous painters.

Take a close look at *Lake Superior*. What do you see? How does it make you feel?

Lake Superior, Lawren Harris.

1. As a class, talk about the lines in this painting:
   a) In what directions do they run?
   b) What is the effect of the arrangement of lines in this painting?
   c) Would you like this painting as well if the trees in the foreground were not there? Why or why not?
   d) What is your reaction to the way Harris has painted the sky?

2. What information and feeling does this painting give you about Lake Superior?

3. You have just become an art critic. Write a short review of Lawren Harris's *Lake Superior* for your classroom magazine.

   Extension: Take your job as art critic more seriously. Write reviews of works of art that you find in your school or community. Try publishing your reviews in your school newspaper or your local community newspaper.

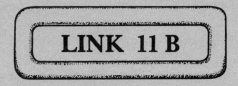

LINK 11 B

In the novel *Who Is Bugs Potter?* the author, Gordon Korman, comes up with some unusual names for rock groups: Migraine, Endomorph, Nuclear Teacup, Winged Tortoise, Dorchester Melon, Plankton, Toast, Spoon Rest, Busted Chandelier.

1. Try making up a name for a rock band.

2. List several in your notebook, and choose the one you like best.

3. Design the logo that would appear on the group's bass drum.

4. Make a class display of these logos.

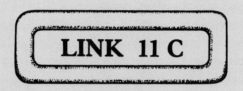

This dictation passage comes from a story about Northern Quebec. Long ago, in the town of L'Enfantville lived two people, Messieur and Madame Gagnon. They had seven marvellous sons, but no daughter. Finally, Madame Gagnon gave birth to a beautiful baby girl. Deliriously happy, M. Gagnon set out to register the birth of his daughter at the Town Hall. But, he gets too much help along the way.

As you write this passage, keep your mind on these skills: spelling, punctuation, paragraphing of dialogue. Watch for these tricky words: off, occurred, dear, there, new and two/to.

According to the custom of L'Enfantville the names of all new babies had to be registered at the Village Hall before the New Year began. Knowing this, Jean set off on the very last day of December to register his new daughter's name.

"Don't forget, my good husband," said Madame, as she waved him goodbye, "don't forget, she is to be called Noëlle because she came to us on Christmas Eve."

"What silliness, wife," Jean replied. "As if I could ever forget such an important thing as that!"

Off he went on his happy task. He did not get far though before it occurred to him that he should share his joy by asking his good friend, Édouard, to accompany him.

G. Joan Morris, "A Tale of Much Rejoicing."

Off M. Jean Gagnon went, to call upon his good friend Édouard, and his good friend Louis, and his good friend Ignace, and Ignace's mother, and on and on, with altogether too much rejoicing.

Extension: Write an ending for this story. What kind of problems does Jean Gagnon create for himself? What will Madame Gagnon think? Compare your ending to that of the original story, if you can find a copy of *The Dancing Sun*.

LINK 11 D

This activity gives you practice reading a short sentence and exploring a number of ways to say it aloud.

1. Practise reading each of the captions for these cartoons on your own:
   a) What tone of voice should you use?
   b) What intonation is required?
   c) Do you want to read them fast or slow? high voice or low?

2. Form groups of two or three. Decide upon the best reading for each caption.

3. Several of the small groups could present their reading in class. As a class, examine the various ways in which these lines have been read.

"I just washed mine, and can't do a thing with it."

"Of course you're going through an identity crisis — you're a chameleon."

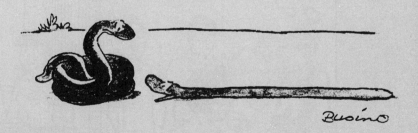

"I had a rough day. I just had to unwind."

EVER NOTICE HOW PEOPLE USE DIFFERENT LABELS WHEN BOYS AND GIRLS DO THE SAME THING---

The DOUBLE STANDARD

WHEN A BOY ATTRACTS GIRLS HE'S "POPULAR"!

---BUT WHEN A GIRL ATTRACTS THE OPPOSITE SEX SHE'S A "FLIRT"!

WHEN A BOY TAKES CHARGE HE HAS "LEADERSHIP ABILITY"!

---WHEN A GIRL TAKES CHARGE SHE'S "BOSSY"!

EDITOR IN CHARGE

WHEN BOYS EXCHANGE NEWS THEY'RE "SHOOTING THE BREEZE"!

WHEN GIRLS EXCHANGE NEWS THEY'RE "GOSSIPING"!

© 1984 Archie Comic Publications Inc.

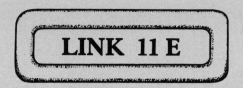

LINK 11 E

1. Make a list of other *double standard* words used for males and females.

2. Do you agree with the argument presented in this comic story?

3. How do you think that double standards begin?

Discussion: What can you do to make certain that there is not a double standard for males and females?

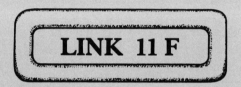

LINK 11 F

Here is another listening exercise.

1. Listen as your teacher reads these lists of numbers for you.

   a) 102   59 38   11
   b)   47 112 24   36
   c)   78   12 92   51   48
   d)   55   34 79   59   6

2. As soon as he or she has finished, write the numbers in your notebook.

3. Make up your own lists of numbers and use them to practise listening. Try to increase the length of the list. Over a period of time you should be able to reach seven numbers, or more. This exercise is good short-term memory training.

4. Make up lists of different items to use for more listening practice: countries, cities, scientific terms, nonsense words. The telephone book is a good source of information: names, numbers, streets.

The Van Bliven Necklace

Mrs Horatio Van Bliven loved caviar and bubble baths and indulged herself accordingly. Part of her hotel room is shown, both before and after the disappearance of her $25,000 necklace.

She said she'd locked her door and taken her bubble bath at seven o'clock, and she denied that the phone had rung, although the operator stated that it had.

The police searched three suspects and their belongings and found nothing. The suspects were: Mrs Van Bliven; Emmy, the pert little chambermaid; and Honore Schmidt, who had an adjacent room that shared Mrs Van Bliven's balcony.

Whom would you arrest for the theft, and what do you think happened to the necklace?

1 Which picture shows the room before the theft?
  a A   b B
2 Was Mrs Van Bliven travelling?
  a Yes   b No
3 What three objects were apparently searched?
4 Is Mrs Van Bliven's denial of receiving a phone call incriminating?
  a Yes   b No

5 Was the pane of glass broken from the outside?
  a Yes   b No
6 Could Schmidt have entered via the French doors?
  a Yes   b No
7 Would Emmy's presence in the room be considered incriminating?
  a Yes   b No
8 Is there evidence that Emmy was in the room?
  a Yes   b No
9 Do you think that Emmy broke the pane of glass?
  a Yes   b No
10 Is it possible that Mrs Van Bliven faked the theft for the insurance money?
  a Yes   b No
11 Where would you look for the necklace?
12 Who stole the necklace?
  a Mrs Van b Emmy   c Schmidt
    Bliven

The solution is on page 211.

Crime and Puzzlement, Lawrence Treat

CHAPTER 11

PETS AND PEOPLE

WHAT'S YOUR POINT OF VIEW?

How would this page look to you if you were only one centimetre tall? You would have a very different point of view if you were suddenly shrunken to a fraction of your size. Some people use the expression *a worm's eye view* to describe the way things would look to such a tiny creature.

How you see something is called your point of view. This chapter tells you about point of view and asks you to take on different points of view as you work your way through the writing process.

Some kinds of writing call for you to look at things the way other people see them. In this story, "The Accident," several people see different parts of the action. When you read the story, watch for the details each of them might notice.

The Accident

Chris was looking forward to almost everything about spending three weeks at summer camp. Plans for camp included hiking, swimming, and canoeing, as well as time for photography, crafts, or music. The only thing Chris was sorry about was leaving Duffy at home.

Duffy was the sleek, black Labrador dog the family had adopted as a puppy almost a year ago. Duffy was much more than just the family pet.

197

You could say that Duffy was Chris's closest friend. The two were always together.

Chris wanted everyone else to admire Duffy too. Chris planned to enter Duffy in the annual dog show at the community centre. The dog show was scheduled to take place the week after summer camp ended. Just before leaving for camp, Chris asked everyone in the family to take good care of Duffy for the next three weeks.

Disaster struck during the second week. Lonely for Chris, Duffy moped around the house, refusing to eat or play. Finally Chris's mother, becoming impatient, decided that Duffy needed some exercise in the back yard and asked Chris's sister Donna to take Duffy outside.

The back yard was enclosed by a high fence with a gate. Donna decided to let Duffy out in the yard first and then find Duffy's leash so they could go for a walk. While she was looking for the leash, the telephone rang. She became so interested in talking to her friend that she forgot all about Duffy.

Just then the newspaper carrier hurried up. After opening the gate and tossing the newspaper on the porch, the carrier was in a hurry to get on to the next house and didn't bother to make sure the gate was shut.

Duffy noticed the carrier dash in and out. It took only a minute for Duffy to follow the carrier through the open gate. Because Duffy was not usually allowed alone in the front yard or on Ranch Parkway, the busy street which ran past the house, everything seemed exciting. Duffy began to bark.

Mr. Horodyski next door was annoyed by the barking and noticed Duffy heading for the street. However, he was busy unloading groceries from his car and didn't want to leave them outside while he took Duffy home. By the time he finished, Duffy was down at the end of the block, and he wasn't sure he could catch the dog. He went inside his house.

In the house at the end of the block lived Sandy, one of Chris's school friends. Sandy, who happened to be watering the lawn when Duffy came along, decided to play one of Duffy's favourite games. Sandy threw a stick for Duffy to chase and carry back. They both became excited as the game went on. Carelessly Sandy began to toss the stick farther and farther, forgetting how busy the street was.

Finally the stick bounced out into the street, with Duffy running right after it. Too late, Sandy saw a delivery truck rounding the corner. The driver was behind schedule and was speeding recklessly to make up lost time. Sandy dashed into the street to call Duffy back, but Duffy bounded right into the truck's path. The driver tried desperately to put on the brakes and avoid the dog. Unfortunately, the truck was going too fast to stop. The front wheel struck Duffy. When Sandy and the truck driver reached Duffy, they found that the dog had a broken front leg and was bleeding from several deep cuts.

Activity 11A   A Chain of Events

In "The Accident," six different people each play a part in the chain of events. Describe who you think is most responsible for what happened to Duffy, and who is least responsible.

1. In your notebook, make up a list of these six names, by arranging them in order from the person you think is most responsible to the person who is least responsible: Mother, Donna, the newspaper carrier, Mr. Horodyski, Sandy, and the truck driver.

2. Be ready to explain your reasons for putting the names in the order you did.

3. Form small groups and explain to each other your reasons for putting the names in the order you did.

4. After each person has explained his or her list, work together to draw up a list that the group agrees upon. Each person should write in his or her notebook.

5. As a class, discuss the reasons for putting the names in the order your group decided on, and draw up a list that everyone in the class can agree with.

"The Way I See It . . ."

You may find that it is not easy to get everyone to agree who is most responsible for Duffy's injuries. Each person may have different ideas about the situation. You could say that everyone will see it in a different way.

The term **point of view** is often used to describe the way people see things. Your point of view about a situation may depend on whether you are the centre of the action or whether you are watching the action from the sidelines. Point of view has several different meanings.

Physical Point of View

Your **physical point of view** means your position in relation to the action. For example, are you in the centre of the action, at the back, or at a lower level looking up? Your physical point of view determines how many details you are able to see. If you miss part of what happens, you might not understand the situation completely. In "The Accident," for example, Mr. Horodyski's physical point of view is limited. From his driveway, he cannot see what is happening to Duffy at the end of the block.

Activity 11B   Physical Point of View

1. In your notebook, make a list of two other people in the story beside Mr. Horodyski who have a limited physical point of view.

2. Explain why each one's physical point of view is limited.

3. Explain how things might be different if their points of view were not limited.

Objective or Subjective Point of View

These terms, **objective** and **subjective point of view,** tell how much your emotions are involved in a situation. An objective point of view means that you stick to the facts only. You do not let your feelings show. On the other hand, a subjective point of view means that you have certain feelings about what you see, like Duffy's feelings about the dog dish in the picture, and those feelings show when you speak or write about the situation.

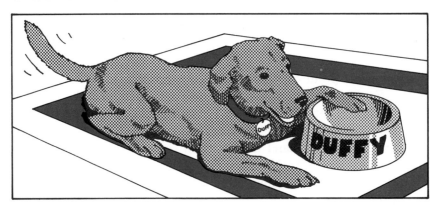

In the story, "The Accident," the writer sometimes takes a subjective point of view. For example, by saying that Sandy *carelessly* tosses the stick for Duffy and that the driver is speeding *recklessly*, the writer is expressing feelings. The expressions do not give you just the facts, such as how far the stick went or how fast the truck was travelling.

Activity 11C   Objective or Subjective Point of View

Look back at "The Accident."

1. **In your notebook, make a list of three other places where the *writer uses a* subjective point of view *to show feelings*.**

2. **Cross out the words that show feelings and rewrite the sentences so they are as objective as possible.**

3. **Be ready to discuss the examples you selected and why you crossed out the words you did.**

Personal Point of View

Personal point of view shows who is telling the story. Sometimes the story tells about a person, using *he* or *she* to refer to the person. The writer is like an observer who can see what is going on but is not directly involved. This is known as **third person point of view**. "The Accident" uses this point of view.

At other times a story may be told as if one of the people involved is talking about himself or herself, using I. In the picture, Duffy is doing this. This is known as **first person point of view**.

This sentence from "The Accident" uses third person point of view to tell about Donna: "She became so interested in talking to her friend that she forgot all about Duffy." If the story switched to first person point of view, Donna would be talking about herself. The sentences might say, "The news about Terry's trip sounded so great that I forgot everything else—until I hung up the phone and realized that I had been talking for twenty minutes with Duffy's leash in my hand."

Activity 11D First Person and Third Person Point of View

1. Pick out one other sentence from "The Accident" that uses third person point of view (he/she) to tell about someone in "The Accident".

2. In your notebook, rewrite the sentence to use first person point of view (I) as if the person is telling about himself or herself.

GET INVOLVED IN THE ACTION

Try putting yourself in someone else's place and using that person's point of view. "The Accident" shows you the entire chain of events leading up to Duffy's injuries. You see events from the point of view of an observer. You are able to follow everything that goes on, but you have not taken part in the action. The following two activities ask you to try to get involved. Choose one.

Activity 11E Telling Chris . . .

Pretend that you are one of the six people who have something to do with Duffy's injuries: Mother, Donna, the newspaper carrier, Mr. Horodyski, Sandy, and the truck driver. For this activity, take the point of view of that person. You are going to write to Chris at the summer camp to explain what happened to Duffy and how you were involved.

1. Write the letter you will send to Chris to break the news. In this letter, tell Chris what happened to Duffy and what you did. *Remember*: Chris cares very much for Duffy and had plans to enter the dog in a dog show.

2. At the *prewriting stage*, you may want to think about the following questions and write answers in your notebook.
   a) What does the person know about the events that happened and the other people who were involved?
   b) Make up a list of the facts about everything leading up to the accident that the person would know.
   c) Make up a list of three new details that the person could add — new information or facts not given in "The Accident," but which would tell more about what the person does or thinks.
   d) Decide whether or not the person would offer to do anything to help make up for what happened.

3. Share these letters as a whole class:
   a) Read each letter aloud, except for the closing signature.
   b) Other students should be able to identify which one of the six people involved in "The Accident" has supposedly written the letter.

Activity 11F   The Media Get Involved

Pretend that you are a reporter for the community weekly newspaper. Ranch Parkway has been the scene of many accidents recently. When you hear that a speeding delivery truck was involved in yet another accident, you decide to write a short report of the accident for the next edition of the community newspaper.

Write the report you will send to the editor of the newspaper. Try to give your readers the most important facts.

A good reporter attempts to use an objective point of view. This means that a good reporter uses facts and tries to keep personal emotions out of the story.

1. Before you write, work by yourself or with your writing partner to gather the facts.

2. At the prewriting stage, you may want to think about the following questions and write down answers in your notebook.
   a) Make a list of all the facts you can gather from "The Accident" that will help you write your report.
   b) Make a list of at least three questions you need to answer before you can write your report.
   For example, you may want to know the name of the truck driver who hit Duffy, although "The Accident" does not tell you.
   c) Let your writing partner take the role of still another resident of Ranch Parkway and provide you with most of your answers.

For example, your writing partner may decide on a name for the truck driver and you can use this detail in your report.

3. Several students who choose this activity may read their reports to the whole class. The other students will listen to decide whether the report includes everything the newspaper readers would want to know. They may ask questions about missing information.

Activity 11G   In Response . . .

As a follow-up to Activity 11E or 11F, take the point of view of another person and write as if you were that person.

1. First, exchange with another student the letter or report you have written for the previous activity.

2. Carefully read the letter or report you have just received and write a short reply to it.

3. If you received a letter addressed to Chris, write the letter you think Chris would send back to that person. (Remember that you are using Chris's point of view for this letter.)

4. If you received a newspaper report, write a letter that you think a concerned pet lover in the neighbourhood would send to the newspaper after reading the report. (Remember to look at the situation from the pet lover's point of view.)

WRITING ABOUT PETS AND PEOPLE

This section suggests some topics for you to write about. Read over the five choices and choose one of them. The suggestions for this writing task are outlined in the next section: The Stages in the Writing Process.

Choice 1:   The Werewolf

You awake suddenly one night, feeling slightly peculiar. The full moon is shining through your window, casting a gray, sickly light over your room. You look down at your arms and hands. Something is wrong! Stringy fur, thick and gray, is sprouting all over your hands and arms.

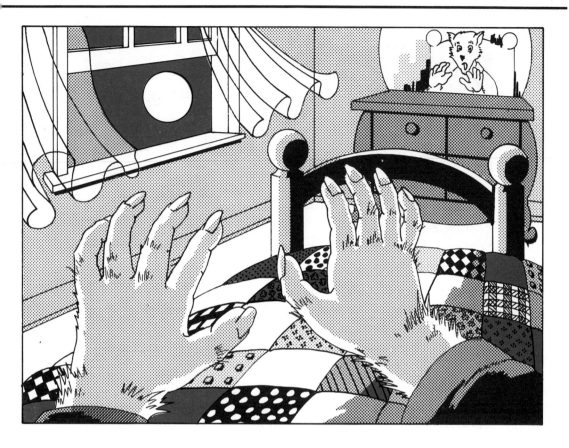

Before your own eyes — you are turning into a werewolf! Strange urges come over you. You scramble to the window, throw it open, and lope off into the black night.

Activity:
Write the story of your adventures that night as a werewolf! Remember, use the point of view of the werewolf, and not your own human self. As a werewolf, tell what you do, what you see and think, and how you feel.

Choice 2: The Toad

You knew very well that the old witch who lives in the woods hates teenagers and now she's proven it — by turning you into a toad! What will you do now? Where can you go? How can you make her turn you back into a teenager?

Activity:
Write the story of the day you spent as a toad.

Remember, a toad is very small and has a different point of view from your usual point of view.

Choice 3: Dracula's Dog

It's a mistake for anyone to think he or she knows all about Dracula! How do I know, you ask. Well, let me tell you. I should know because I am Dracula's watch dog. I've been guarding this castle for fifteen years. And I've seen some strange sights, I tell you. Why, just the other day, as the wind was howling, and the black clouds swirled across the dark sky, hiding the light of the moon. . .

Activity:

Write the story of what you do and see during a day and a night as Dracula's watch dog. You will really be able to tell what it means *to live a dog's life*.

Remember, you are limited to what you see and hear, as a dog who is standing guard outside the castle.

Choice 4: The Planet Zoltar

You are a traveller by nature. Ever since you were a small child, you have been a wanderer. Do you remember when you were two years old, the time you scared us all silly by driving off on your sister's trike? Well you've done it again. But this time you've gone too far!

It was a hot summer noon, in mid-July. You were walking home from the ball field. An alien ship landed on the road in front of you. Zap. A shot rang out. You were paralyzed. You couldn't move or talk, but you could still hear everything.

Two greenish, yellow aliens jumped out of the space ship, and scooped you up.

And here you are on the planet Zoltar, locked in a cage: the main exhibit in the Zoltar Zoo. "Come see the human creature from the planet Earth!"

Activity:

Write the story of what you do during a day at the zoo and how you make plans to get back to Earth.

Remember, although you are still a human being, your physical point of view is limited to what you can observe from your cage.

207

Choice 5: The Zoo on Earth

Have you ever gone to a zoo? If so, you probably have had some fascinating times. It's fun to see the strange animals—the elephants and tigers, llamas and ostriches.

But a zoo can be a sad place, too. How do the animals feel? What do they think, as they pace up and down, up and down, behind steel bars and high wire fences?

Some zoo animals are born in captivity. Others are captured wild, and placed in cages, just so that you can look at them in zoos and parks.

Activity:
Imagine that you are a zoo animal—a polar bear, an elephant, a tiger. Write the story of a day of your life in your cage. Remember, you have to take the point of view of the animal you have picked. Your physical point of view is limited to what you can see from your cage. But you do have a memory and an imagination.

THE STAGES IN THE WRITING PROCESS

This section will help you write the story you chose from the last section: the werewolf, the toad, Dracula's dog, Zoltar's zoo, or the Earth zoo.

You will find it easier to do this writing task if you proceed through the stages of the writing process.

Activity 11H   Prewriting

Before you choose a project, discuss the suggestions that follow with a group of other students. After you are finished talking about these choices of topics, you may be able to use some of the group's ideas to help build your own story.

Your class should divide into writing groups of four or five students. You do not have to choose the same writing project. You can gain ideas from each other as you discuss the possibilities of each of the five writing choices.

You will probably find it easiest to talk about one choice at a time, as you go through the possibilities of the five topics.

1. How would you feel if you were the creature in each of the choices?

2. List three things that you might do if you were the creature.

3. Note at least one thing that you would avoid doing, as the creature.

4. Which of the five different choices do you think is the easiest to imagine?

5. For each of the choices, decide whether it is better to tell the story using the point of view *I* or the point of view *he/she*.

Activity 11I   Writing

Decide upon a point of view for your story, and then write the story from that point of view. At this stage in the writing process, you may want to concentrate on using all the details you think will fit your story.

Do not worry about whether everything is completely correct. You can go back later and polish your writing to make it as good as possible. Your writing partner can help you with suggestions during the proofreading and editing stage.

Activity 11J   Revising and Rewriting

Share the first draft of your story with a writing partner. You can help each other by writing comments such as these:

1. Point out any place in the story where the details belong to your usual point of view as a human being, rather than your point of view as the creature in your story.

2. Ask two questions about something the character mentions that you want to know more about.

3. Suggest one more thing the character in the story might do in that particular situation.

4. Suggest the words that could be added to the story to show feelings or emotions.

Revise your story as needed. Include any extra details that will help build up the character's point of view. Look carefully at your writing partner's suggestions and decide whether or not you want to use them.

Activity 11K   Editing and Proofreading

Exchange your story with your writing partner one more time. This time your task is to help each other with the mechanics of the story, rather than the ideas, so that you can prepare the piece of writing to share with others.

You can help each other by checking for these things:

1. Pick out any sentence in which the meaning is unclear.

2. Point out any place where the personal point of view shifts from first person (I) to third person (he/she).

3. Check to see if you can find any misspelled words.

4. Check to see if the punctuation marks at the end of each sentence are right.

Write your final copy.

Activity 11L   Publishing and Sharing

It's time now to share your creation with others. Here are some suggestions. You will be able to think of others:

1. Invite a guest for a sharing session where students in your class read their stories aloud. Think of good sound effects and lighting to go along with your stories. (To get some eerie lighting, try putting a little cooking oil and some food colouring in a clear pie or cake pan. Set it on the overhead projector, and swirl just a little.)

2. Publish a class collection of animal stories. Write a class introduction to your collection. Be sure to note what you learned about point of view and how this collection shows your skills in handling point of view. Indeed, you might even put stories into sections according to their point of view.

3. **Have each group of students suggest one way to use the best stories in order to make people kinder to animals.**

The Point of All This

In this chapter, you have experimented with different points of view as you worked your way through the writing process. Next time you think about a topic, think carefully about the point of view you could choose. The point of view you use to describe or explain your subject will affect the way your reader sees it.

Solution to the Van Bliven Necklace

1 A, because the clock indicates an earlier time than in B.
2 Yes, because her suitcase is out.
3 The jewel box (open), the dresser drawer (open), and the suitcase (moved with one of the catches left open).
4 No, because she would not have heard the phone ring while it was unplugged.
5 No, because the broken glass lies outside the room.
6 No, only if he had broken a window from the inside of Mrs Van Bliven's room to unlock the doors, which would have been impossible.
7 No. She had legitimate reasons for entering the room, such as bringing towels and turning down the bed.
8 Yes, because the bed is turned down.
9 No. If she had stolen the necklace, she would have avoided making any noise or leaving evidence of her presence.
10 Yes. She could easily have manufactured all the evidence present.
11 In the vase, because the flowers were moved, and there seems to have been no other reason for rearranging or tampering with them.
12 Mrs Van Bliven, because we have eliminated the other two suspects, and she could have recovered the necklace from the vase at any time she wished. Due to her craving for caviar and the money she'd spent for it, she was badly in need of cash. 'Caviar was my downfall!' she cried out as she was led away by the police.

LINK 12 A

This bridge activity requires you to look at some photographs and to create a story about them.

1

1. Look at photograph 1 and record the first word that comes into your mind about it.

2. Use this word as the centre for a thought web about this photograph. (Review instructions for thought webs in Link 2.)

3. Follow the same procedures for photograph 2 and photograph 3.

4. Choose the photograph that you like best. Use the thought web you made for that photograph to write a paragraph of eight or ten sentences. Next, look at your paragraph to decide which point of view you used to write it: physical, objective, subjective, third person, first person. Then, rewrite your paragraph from another point of view.

Extension: Form writing pairs. Working together, construct a paragraph that tells a story about all of the photographs. This story must contain details from each of the three photographs.

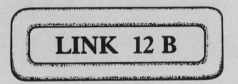

LINK 12 B

Here is another activity about point of view. Read the newspaper on the following page. It is written by a newspaper reporter, with an objective point of view.

1. Form writing groups of four or five students.

2. Select one of the following writing starters and write another account of the story of the boy under the bridge:
   a) the boy telling his father later in the day
   b) the boy telling his cousin, one week later

c) the boy's friend telling the rest of the gang
d) the police sergeant telling the office staff
e) the spokesperson from the Fire Department reporting to his or her supervisor

Note: In doing this writing task, you are changing this account from the objective point of view of the newspaper article to the subjective point of view of someone retelling the story.

Boy slips from tight squeeze

A Saskatoon youngster who found himself in a slippery situation will probably be a little more cautious the next time he decides to be adventurous.

The boy, 7, and a friend were under the Idylwyld Freeway river about noon Friday and were making their way through the concrete abutments when the child got his head caught, according to a Fire Department spokesman.

Police were called and took their boat out but the boy was nowhere near the water. The Fire Department's rescue unit was called.

His head was lubricated with vehicle grease to cut down the friction, but it still took 20 minutes to free the boy.

He was taken to hospital for observation and later released. He had no serious injuries, a Fire Department spokesman said.

Saskatoon *Star-Phoenix*

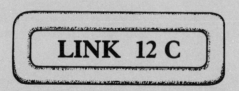

LINK 12 C

This dictation passage reviews many of the skills of spelling, punctuation, and paragraphing.

September 5, 1980, was an important day for Marta Mitchell. On this day she started school. Her mother took her to Central Elementary School, which is located in Brandon, Manitoba.

The day passed slowly for Mrs. Mitchell. When Marta returned home, she looked sad and dejected.

"I hate school!" Marta announced defiantly.

"Why, Marta!" exclaimed Mrs. Mitchell. "Tell me your troubles."

"I haven't received my present yet," Marta started. "I waited for it all day, too."

"A present! What present?" questioned Mrs. Mitchell.

Little Marta innocently said, "Mr. Taylor told me to sit in my desk for the present, and I sat all day and didn't receive anything."

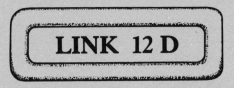

LINK 12 D

Poundmaker was a powerful leader of the Cree Indians in Western Canada during the time of Louis Riel. Poundmaker was brought to trial for leading his followers against the Eastern Canadian forces. Here is the speech he made during his trial.

1. Read Poundmaker's speech over quickly to get a feel for the whole passage.

2. Decide how this passage should be read. Remember you are reading the words of a stately Indian chief.

3. Four or five members of the class should deliver Poundmaker's speech.

4. As a class, discuss each reading. Look for the good things that occur in each reading.

> I am not guilty. A lot has been said against me that is untrue. I am glad of what I have done in the Queen's country. What I did was for the Great Mother. When my people and the whites met in battle, I saved the Queen's men. I took the firearms from my following and gave them up at Battleford. Everything I could do was to prevent bloodshed. Had I wanted war, I would not be here but on the prairie. You did not catch me. I gave myself up. You have me because I wanted peace. I cannot help myself, but I am still a man. You may do as you like with me.
>
> Hugh A. Dempsey, *Crowfoot: Chief of the Blackfeet*

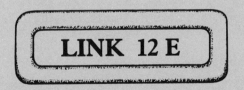

LINK 12 E

The small ad on the next page contains several errors.

1. Proofread it and rewrite the ad in your notebook. Look for spelling errors particularly.

Everyone must proofread his or her work. Otherwise unwanted errors creep in, as they did in this ad.

CITY BADMINTOR CLUB

16 Spadina West (Vistio Park)   123-6543

THIS VOUCHER GOOD FOR

Free   Free

ONE (1) EVENING OF COURT TIME FOR
TO PEOPLE
(VALUE $10.00)

Please phone for backing procedure

This Offer Expires APRIL 10.   **Authorized By**
                                             Roy Smith

LINK 12 F

You are a secret agent, working for the Canadian government in Paris. You have been assigned to a difficult case. After six months work, you collected all of the data you needed. You wrote your report and stored it in your hotel room. To avoid theft, you hid your report in four boxes. But curses! Someone broke into your room and stole your packages, and a lot of other things.

Now you are sitting in a Paris metro station. Over the top of a lot of conversation you hear the following talk, quite by accident. It must be the thieves who stole your report. They seem to be telling each other where they hid your packages.

1. Your teacher will select two students to read the following conversation in a normal tone, at a normal speed.

2. Listen carefully to this conversation to hear the locker numbers and combinations of the locks. Your report is hidden there.

3. When the dialogue is finished, pick up your pen and write down the locker numbers and lock combinations without looking at your text.

How good are you at hearing and remembering numbers? Will you get a job with the Secret Service?

Matilda: Did ya get the goods, Spike?

Spike: Ya, Matilda. It was as easy as takin' candy from a baby.

Matilda: Did ya hide it good? We can't be too careful in this business, you know.

Spike: Ya, Matilda. I hid it. Maybe we should tell each other what we done wid da goods, joist in case, eh?

Matilda: I hid me packages in a locker in this station. And you?

Spike: Me, too. What a coincidence, eh Boss? Should we, like, trade coimbinations, just in case, like a body can't be too careful in this business, eh Boss?

Matilda: OK, Spike, ya got a good idea for onest. Youse gotta tell me yours foist. I'll write da coimbination on my wrist. Ya ready?

Spike: OK, Boss, here's the foist one. Da coimbination is 11, 37, 57. (Pause.) Ya got dat? (Matilda nods.) De locker number is 3-7-8. (Pause.)

Matilda: Yeh, Spike. Go on!

Spike: OK, da second is in Locker 34. (Pause.) Da coimbination is 26, 51, 42. (Pause.) Is dat OK, Boss?

Matilda: Right, Spike. I got ya. Now for moine! I put my packages in Locker 92 (pause) and the coimbination is 45, 3, 67. (Pause.) OK, Spike? Da other package is in Locker 8 (pause) and the coimbination is 69, 53, 9. (Pause.)

Spike: We done a good job, eh Boss? Let's go grab a cup o' coiffee.

Untitled, Jessie Oonark

CHAPTER 12

WAITER! . . .
ALLIGATOR STEW, PLEASE

Have you ever been to a high-school sports tournament? There the cheerleaders put on a performance as impressive as that of the players.

> We've got the T-E-A-M
> That's on the B-E-A-M.
>
> You can beat your eggs,
> You can whip your cream
> But you can't beat
> Central's volleyball team!

And then the crowd gets fired up:

> Go, team, go!
> Go! Go! Go! . . . . CHARGE!

There's something exciting about a group of people chanting together. No matter whether it's a school game or the Grey Cup final, crowds have their special oral rituals. It's a part of life.

This chapter is about speaking together. It's about something that is a special part of all people. You will experience the magic, not of chanting a school yell, but of performing a literary work. And you may gain something more. If you follow the activities in this chapter, you will practise the skills needed to be a good speaker. This ability will help you when you have to speak in public.

Practice One: Unison Work

In this practice session, you will learn to present Dennis Lee's "Alligator Pie" as a choral reading. First, it will be necessary to do some warm-up exercises to help you speak clearly and distinctly.

Activity 12A   Warm-ups   1

1. **As a class, read these tongue twisters. You may want to come back to this exercise later, to see if you can increase the speed or rate with which you read these tongue twisters. If your words become garbled, decrease the pace of your reading.**
   a) **Read each tongue twister slowly and deliberately the first time, saying the words clearly and carefully.**
   b) **Read each tongue twister two more times.**

> The sixth sheik's sixth sheep's sick.
> The Leith police dismisseth us.
> Sixty-six thick thistle sticks.

2. **As a class, practise these exercises to gain flexibility of your lips. Read each list of words three times, as directed:**

List 1	List 1
hub-bub	a) *first time* — slowly, normal voice tone
dib-dab	b) *second time* — more quickly, normal voice tone
dabble	c) *third time* — very rapidly, normal voice tone
babble	
bubble	

List 2	List 2
pip	a) *first time* — very slowly, softly
pop	b) *second time* — louder, more quickly
pippin	c) *third time* — very loudly, quickly
piping	
piper	

3. **As a class, do this activity to practise the rhythm of choral speaking:**
   a) **Clap your hands in time and recite the following patter exercise. Clap only *four* beats to each line:**

   > Mumbo Jumbo
   > Christopher Columbo
   > I'm sitting on the sidewalk
   > Chewing bubble gumbo.
   >
   > Dennis Lee

   b) **Redo this patter exercise. Move your bodies to the rhythm. Sway from side to side as you recite in a brisk manner.**
   c) **Redo this patter exercise one more time. Snap your fingers as you recite the selection.**

Activity 12B   Alligator Pie

Now you are ready to tackle "Alligator Pie," by Dennis Lee:

Alligator Pie

Alligator pie, alligator pie,
If I don't have some I think I'm gonna die.
Give away the green grass, give away the sky.
But don't give away my alligator pie.

Alligator stew, alligator stew,
If I don't get some I don't know what I'll do.
Give away my furry hat, give away my shoe,
But don't give away my alligator stew.

Alligator soup, alligator soup,
If I don't get some I think I'm gonna droop.
Give away my hockey-stick, give away my hoop,
But don't give away my alligator soup.

Dennis Lee

Your class should divide into three groups:

a) *Group A:*
   Chant the phrase "alligator stew" softly four times, at which

point Group B will chime in with some rhythm instruments. Without pausing, Group A continues to chant "alligator stew" throughout the course of the poem.

Group B:
After the fourth time that Group A chants "alligator stew" you will join in by tapping on rhythm instruments like triangles, bells, and drums in keeping with the rhythm that Group A has set. Keep this pace for the next four counts at which point Group C will join in by reciting the whole poem. Group B is to continue playing on the rhythm instruments throughout the selection.

Group C:
When Group A and B have chanted and played the rhythm instruments to eight counts, Group C chimes in by reciting the whole selection. Groups A, B, and C perform the selection twice without pausing, in the same manner as one would perform a singing round.

b) Variation
Group A: on rhythm instruments
Group B: chants the whole selection
Group C: chants "alligator soup"

c) Variation
Try making up new stanzas and recite them in a manner described in (a).
Example:
Brontosaurus cake, brontosaurus cake
If I don't get some I think I'm gonna break.
Give away my grasshopper, give away my snake,
But don't give away my brontosaurus cake.

d) Now try sound effects that go with your verse and reading. Can you make visuals for an overhead projector to suggest the mood of your poem?

Practice Two: Two-Part or Antiphonal Poems

In this section, you will learn to present "Doctor, Doctor" as a choral arrangement. This is an example of an **antiphonal** arrangement, meaning that two kinds of voices present this poem as a dialogue. Right now, it's time to do some warm-ups to get ready for "Doctor, Doctor."

Activity 12C   Warm-ups 2

1. This activity will help you achieve flexibility in voice tone, or your ability to raise or lower the sound of your voice.
   a) Say no in each of the following ways, as a whole class or in small groups.

No!	(I absolutely refuse.)
No!	(It can't be true.)
No!	(I'm disgusted.)
No!	(Now, that isn't amusing.)
No!	(That's not the idea exactly, but perhaps you'll get it in a minute.)

   b) Say oh in each of the following ways, individually or in small groups.

Oh!	(as if someone stepped on your foot)
Oh!	(as if you are very sleepy)
Oh!	(as if the dentist's drill hit a nerve)
Oh!	(as if you are tasting an ice cream cone on a hot summer day)
Oh!	(as if you are biting into something that tastes bitter)
Oh!	(as if you had a failing report card to take home)
Oh!	(as if you lost your temper)
Oh!	(as if you are petting your dog or cat)
Oh!	(as if you are swinging like Tarzan from one jungle vine to the next)

2. Practise shifting emphasis in the following exercise:
   a) Yes, I like him.   (No doubt about it.)
      Yes, I like him.   (Someone else doesn't).
      Yes, I like him.   (But there are some reservations.)
      Yes, I like him.   (But certainly not his cousin).
   b) Put the accent or stress on a different word in each of these sentences each time you read them. What is the effect of the change in emphasis?
      You come here now.
      I love you.
      Call my parents.
      The boat is sinking.
      This is my sister.

3. As your teacher counts from one to fifteen, in unison with other class members:
   a) Yell out Hi on the odd numbers in these tones: happily, sadly, haughtily.
   b) Yell out Hi on the even numbers in these tones: stunned, irritably, sternly.

4. Count from one to ten in the following ways:
   a) as if you are counting people in a crowded room
   b) as if your are counting pennies on the table
   c) as if you are counting out a man in a boxing ring
   d) as if you are counting off in an exercise routine

5. Tell three short stories — serious, funny, mysterious — using the letters of the alphabet instead of words. Have the feeling, as you do this exercise, that you are playing with tones.

6. You and your partner carry on an animated conversation with each other, with the rest of the class watching, by using gibberish. When you talk in gibberish, you use nonsense, make-believe words, but you make the normal tones of natural speech.

   If you find it difficult at first to think up non-words, use only the phrase *da-da-shoon*. Sincerely try to communicate with each other.

7. By varying the inflection, or the highness and lowness of your voice, you can talk with the alphabet and capture the feeling indicated in parentheses:

   a) ABC   (A question)
   b) DEF   (Please!)
   c) GHI   (Oh, why not?)
   d) JKL   (Are you quite sure?)
   e) MN   (So that's it!)
   f) O   (So what.)
   g) PQRST   (All right! Have it your way.)
   h) UV   (You don't think so?)
   i) WXYZ   (I never ever want to see you again.)

8. Sometimes inflection can give rise to vocal double-dealing or double entendre. Words inflected one way seem sincere. Another inflection gives them the opposite meaning.

   Say the following, first sincerely, then sarcastically:
   a) Some hairdo!
   b) I'll give you a hand.
   c) She's beautiful.
   d) You don't say so!

e) That's some hat!
f) You've certainly lost weight.

Now you are ready to start work on *"Doctor, Doctor."*

Activity 12D   Doctor, Doctor

1. a) Listen as your teacher, or another student, reads the poem aloud.
   b) As a whole class, read this poem in unison to get a feeling for it.

2. Your class should divide into groups. Group A should contain the dark voices and Group B the light voices.
   Note: Most boys will have dark voices and most girls will have light voices.

3. Use the notes in the margin to interpret "Doctor, Doctor."

   Group B:
   Try to make your voices light and amused.
   Group A:
   You will have to express concern in various tones. Pretend you are doing an old-time vaudeville act. The lines must be said quite quickly or else the poem loses its tongue-in-cheek humour.

4. Play with the inflection and tone — the highness and lowness in your voice. Stress different words for effect. Remember the speech exercises you tried earlier were designed to prepare you for this selection.

   Group A:
   Try saying "Doctor, Doctor" in different tones. Then decide on three different tones and maintain them throughout the poem.

   Group B:
   Try accenting different words. For example, the first time round, accent *one* as in *"One* at a time, please!" Then, accent *time* the next try round, and then *please* when you try the line on the third time. See which effect you think is most desirable and keep to it. Do the same thing with the other lines.

5. Read the poem with the tones and inflectional patterns decided upon.

Doctor, Doctor

Group A: Accent *two*	Doctor, doctor, I keep thinking there's two of me.''
Group B: Accent *please*	"One at a time, please!"
Group A: Accent *I*	"Doctor, doctor, I keep thinking I'm a garbage can."
Group B: Accent *rubbish*	"Oh, don't talk such rubbish!"
Group A: Accent *cards*	"Doctor, doctor, I feel like a pack of cards."
Group B: Accent *deal*	"Wait and I'll deal with you later."
Group A: Accent second *doctor*	"Doctor, doctor, I feel like a spoon."
Group B: Accent *don't*	"Sit down, and don't stir."
Group A: Accent *strawberry*	"Doctor, doctor, I keep thinking I'm a strawberry."
Group B: Accent *really*	"Oh, dear, you're really in a jam, aren't you!"
Group A: Accent second *doctor*	"Doctor, doctor, I feel like a pair of drapes."
Group B: Accent *pull*	"Well, pull yourself together then!"
Group A: Accent *clock*	"Doctor, doctor, I keep thinking I'm a clock."
Group B: Accent *woundup*	"Well, don't get woundup about it."
Group A: Accent *feel*	"Doctor, doctor, I feel like a dollar bill."
Group B: Accent *change'll*	"Go shopping, the change'll do you good."
Group A: Accent *everyone*	"Doctor, doctor, everyone thinks I'm a liar."
Group B: Accent *I*	"Really, I don't believe you."
Group A: Accent *please*	"Doctor, doctor, please will you help me out?"
Group B: Accent *Sure*	"Sure. Which way did you come in?"

Meguido Zola

Practice Three: Sequential Work

This practice session gives you the skill to read the short poem, "Orders." This poem will be read in **sequence**. That is, one person will read a line, followed by another, and so on until you reach the last line of the poem. It will be read in unison as a conclusion. But first, some warm-ups!

Activity 12E Warm-ups 3

1. This exercise will help you develop flexibility with your tongue:
   a) Place the tip of your tongue behind your upper teeth.
   b) On the count of *one*, bulge your tongue by pressing it against your top teeth.

c) On the count of *two*, relax.

d) Repeat this exercise eight times.

2. Try this exercise to increase voice projection. *Projection* means the skill of extending your voice so that it can be heard at a distance.

What does it mean to project your voice? You need varying degrees of strength or volume in daily communication as you speak with others. A telephone conversation calls for a small amount of energy, but calling a taxicab, or cheering at a game, may be a test of your projective power. An efficient voice is not loud, but it has sufficient volume to make certain that every member of an audience, no matter how large the room, hears without strain. Shouting is ineffective. Try to speak loudly without straining.

a) Project the following phrases across a large room and bounce them off the opposite wall. Project. Don't simply increase your loudness.

Ship Ahoy! Ship Ahoy!
Hello down there!
Boomlay, boomlay, boomlay, BOOM!

b) Repeat this exercise in small groups and again as a whole class.

3. Use this next exercise to practise controlling the speed of your speaking.

a) Read these sentences slowly, decreasing the speed within each sentence:

The leaves dropped one by one from the branches.
The cat burglar crept slowly, so very slowly, till she came to the bottom of the creaky stairway.

Now. Let's begin reading "Orders."

Activity 12F   Orders

1. Read "Orders" as directed by the notes in the margin.

2. After you and your class have mastered this reading, experiment with other ways to read the poem.

Orders

Solo 1:	annoyed	Muffle the wind;
Solo 2:	harsh	Silence the clock;
Solo 3:	worried	Muzzle the mice;
Solo 4:	sarcastic	Curb the small talk;
Solo 5:	annoyed	Cure the hinge-squeak;
Solo 6:	angry	Banish the thunder.
Unison:	slowly	Let me sit silent.
Unison:	Slowly and softly, hold on *wonder*	Let me wonder.

A.M. Klein

3. **You will have to work on the problems created by sequential reading.**

   a) **Each speaker will have to keep up the pitch of his or her voice at the end of each line, so that each line leads to the main thought:**

   Let me sit silent./Let me wonder.

   b) **Speakers must make sure that there are no long pauses at the end of each line delivered, or the thought of the poem will seem disconnected and it will be hard to understand your reading.**

Practice Four: Three-Part Poems

This section leads to the choral reading of "Waiter! . . . There's an Alligator in My Coffee." Right now, it's time to do some warm-ups to get ready for "Waiter!"

Activity 12G Warm-ups 4

1. **Try to avoid a nasal sound in choral reading. A nasal sound is one which seems to come out of your nose. Here is an exercise to help avoid nasality:**

   a) **Pinch your nostrils and read these sentences as a whole class. There should be no change in the quality of the sound during your reading.**

   Ruth cut up the fish swiftly.
   The rude pup roughed up the rug.
   Bobby bought a buttered duck.
   The butcher hooked a cookie.
   Sue bought a box of dull books.

b) **Without pinching your nostrils, read this next set of sentences as a whole class. You should keep the same quality of sound that you produced in the first set.**

> Banging, clanging hair-raising gongs rang deafeningly to warn the remaining gangs.
> The mangled remains of mammals make many museums memorable.
> "Ouch!" he shouted as he bowed and backed into the mouse trap.
> Joe Blow, the local show-off, posed as a rider at the rodeo.
> The cook forsook the book to look at the rook who was hooking a cookie.

c) **Read these sets of sentences again, reversing the order. Read the first set without pinching your nostrils, and the second set with nostrils pinched. Listen for the quality of sound that you produce.**

2. **You can strengthen weak-sounding tones in your choral speaking. To do this, speak the following words with enthusiasm. Try this first in pairs, and then as a whole class. Hint: *Think of a situation that would make each word natural before speaking it.***

excellent	ours	voices
marvellous	free	beat
safe	treasure	food
victory	keys	

3. **The rate, or speed, with which you speak helps communicate meaning. Some sentences should be read rapidly and others, slowly.**

a) **As a class, read each of these sentences first rapidly and then slowly. Exaggerate the reading, just to get a stronger feeling for the way your speed of reading changes the meaning.**

b) **After reading each sentence rapidly and slowly, analyze your reading. Answer these questions: What is the effect of rate of speaking on the message that is communicated? Describe a situation in which you would be likely to say each of these sentences.**

> It was long, long ago.
> She dreamed gently all night.
> Please keep still a moment.

There it is!
They were old and thin and worn.
My! But it's hot today.
The dawn was hushed and lovely.
Get out of my sight!
The stream murmurs sad songs.

Now you are reading for "Waiter! . . . There's an Alligator in My Coffee!"

Activity 12H Waiter!

1. **To get ready for this three-part reading, do this activity:**
   a) **Listen as your teacher, or another student, reads the poem aloud.**
   b) **As a whole class, read the poem in *unison* to get a feeling for it.**

2. **Divide the class into three groups, A, B, and C.**
   Group A could have light voices, Group B, dark voices, and Group C could portray the middle-sounding voices. A solo voice could be used in place of Group C.

3. **Use the notes in the margin to interpret "Waiter! . . . There's an Alligator in My Coffee!" These notes are only a guide. You may wish to interpret parts of the poem differently in following readings.**

Waiter! . . . There's an Alligator in My Coffee

Group A:	astonished accent *alligator*	Waiter! . . . there's an alligator in my coffee.
Group B:	sarcastically	Are you trying to be funny? he said: what do you want for a dime . . . ? . . . a circus?
Group A:	insistently	but sir! I said, he's swimming around in my coffee and he might jump out on the table . . .
Group B:	angrily	Feed him a lump of sugar! he snarled — no! . . . make it two; it'll weigh him down and he'll drown.

Group A:		I dropped two blocks of sugar
		into the swamp,
	clipped	two grist jaws snapped them up
	diction	and the critter —
	surprised tone	he never drowned.
	desperately	Waiter! . . . there's an alligator in my coffee.
Group B:	emphasize	Kill him! Kill him!
	second *kill*	he said:
		BASH HIS BRAINS OUT
		WITH YOUR SPOON . . .
Group C:	casually	What seems to be the trouble:
		The owner inquired,
Group A:	firm tones	and I replied:
	emphasize *my coffee*	There's an alligator in my coffee!
Group C:	unconcerned	. . . But the coffee's fresh, he said
		and raised the cup to his nose . . .
Group A:	cautiously	Careful! I said,
		he'll bite it
		off
Group C:	sarcastically	and he replied:
		How absurd,
		and lowered the cup
		level to his mouth and
		swallowed
		the profit motive.

Joe Rosenblatt

Practice Five: On Your Own

This section contains one more poem for choral speaking.

Activity 12I   A Canadian Poem

1. **Read E. J. Pratt's poem, ''The Shark'' as scored (or indicated by the directions) in the textbook.**

2. **When you have mastered this choral rendition, develop your own score for ''The Shark.''**

	The Shark (Unison)
casual	He seemed to know the harbour,
	So leisurely he swam;
	His fin,
	Like a piece of sheet-iron,
	Three-cornered,
sinister overtones	And with knife edge,
smoothly	Stirred not a bubble
unruffled tones	As it moved
	With its base-line on the water.
slowly	His body was tubular
measured tones	And tapered
	And smoke-blue,
faster	And as he passed the wharf
	He turned,
staccato	And snapped at a flat-fish
	That was dead and floating.
grim, fearful	And I saw the flash of a white throat,
build tempo	And a double row of white teeth,
implacable, faster	And eyes of metallic gray,
menacing, slower	Hard and narrow and slit.
leisurely	Then out of the harbour,
	With that three-cornered fin,
smoothly	Shearing without a bubble the water
	Lithely,
	Leisurely,
	He swam —
emphasize *strange*	That strange fish,

amazement	Tubular, tapered, smoke-blue,
surprise	Part vulture, part wolf,
hold *blood*	Part neither — for his blood was cold.
cold, sinister tones	

E.J. Pratt

Curtain Call

The chapter comes to an end, but your experiences with choral speaking need not. You can use your skills in many ways. You can add choral reading as an extra to your literature class. Why not select some literary works from your textbook and put on a choral reading session? Invite the class next door. Better still, use choral reading as a means to publish your own writing.

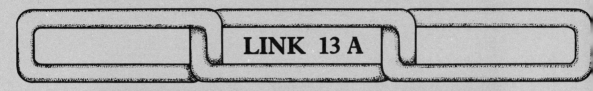

LINK 13 A

Northern Lights Frank H. Johnston

Northern Lights hangs in the National Art Gallery in Ottawa. After looking at it for a few moments, work at these questions:

1. As a whole class, talk about your thoughts as you examined this painting.
   a) Why are the two men so small?
   b) What are they thinking?
   c) Why are the trees so tall?
   d) How do the lines work in this painting? How do they make you feel?

2. Does this painting make you think of some other painting or short story or TV program? What? Why?

3. On your own, construct a thought web to organize your thoughts about *Northern Lights*.

4. Use your thought web to write a paragraph about this painting. Here is a possible title for your paragraph: "Northern Lights and Me."

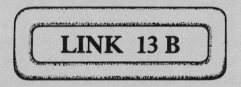

LINK 13 B

This dictation passage was selected from the adolescent novel, *Jady and the General*. Twelve-year-old Jady lives on a peach farm near Niagara-on-the-Lake in southern Ontario. In this passage, he faces the prospect of his first crop failure.

Jady could not believe it! No peaches! This had never happened in his lifetime that he could remember. Oh, he knew there was always the fear of it, always the anxious consulting of weather reports in the paper, and the close attention to every detail of the weather news on the radio. And then when the spring season was safely past and the summer launched, there was always the noticeable easing of tension. His father knew that in summer there were only parasites and diseases to fight in the trees, things that he could do something about with all the new scientific knowledge from the government and the Experimental Farm.

Lyn Cook, *Jady and the General*

LINK 13 C

These signs were developed for the 1964 Olympic Games in Toyko, Japan.

1. Use them as a model.

2. Develop signs that you could use around your school to show where different school activities occur: the stage, the music room, the art room, the gym, the staff room.

Gymnastics   Swimming   Soccer

LINK 13 D

a)

"Who's the clown going 'beep beep'?
Doesn't he know we're honkers?"

b)

"When I think of all those winters we wasted
hibernating in that stupid cave . . . !"

1. On your own, decide how the captions for these cartoons might be read.

2. As a class, try out several ways of saying these captions.

3. Decide which way is best and look for reasons to support your decision.

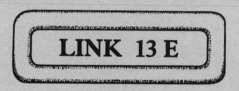

LINK 13 E

Use these questions as thought starters for a class discussion of the cartoons in Link 13 D.

1. Look at the first cartoon.
   a) What does it mean to be a *honker*? a *beeper*?
   b) Is it easier to be a *honker* or a *beeper*? Why?
   c) What would happen if everyone were a *beeper*? a *honker*?
   d) Think about some of the prominent politicians in your area and classify them as *honkers* or *beepers*.
   e) Look at several magazine ads. Are the people displayed in these ads *honkers* or *beepers*? How do you know?
   f) Watch several situation comedy programs on television. Are the main characters in these programs *honkers* or *beepers*? How do you know this?

2. Look at the second cartoon.
   a) Did the bears really waste time hibernating in a cave? Why or why not?
   b) Do·you know anyone who has wasted time "hibernating in a stupid cave"? What did they do?
   c) Have you wasted any time "hibernating in a stupid cave"? How?

3. Construct a thought web for these cartoons to summarize your class discussion of them.

Extension: Make a bulletin board display of cartoons or short comic strip stories. Write one or two sentences beside each cartoon or comic strip to show how it connects with everyday life.

Whale Sound S. Mogensen

CHAPTER 13

Maybe I Will . . . Then Again

Decisions! Decisions! Decisions! You make them all the time. You make some decisions without thinking about them, while others cause you to struggle to find your answer.

This chapter will look at decisions and help you understand the way you go about making them. You will learn some basic steps that you can use to help you make decisions. You will also learn how to write an argument based upon the decisions you make.

Activity 13A Me . . . Make Decisions?

Here's an easy activity to get you started:

1. In your notebook, list three decisions that you made today.

2. For each one, write down a different choice you might have made.

3. Next, write down the reason you had for making each of your decisions and for not choosing your alternate choice.

4. As a class, talk about *how* you went about making your decisions:
   a) Did you make your choices without thinking about them?
   b) Do you have a method or system that you used to help make your decisions?

WHAT IS A DECISION?

Here are Lance   and Sonja

The next activities will get you to think about their decisions so that you can better understand your own decisions.

Activity 13B Lance and Sonja's Simple Decisions

Study each of these pictures and then answer the following questions in your notebook:

1. What decisions did Lance make?

2. What other choices could he have made?

3. What decisions did Sonja make?

4. What other decisions could she have made?

These are easy decisions. Here is something a little harder to answer.

> **Lance and Sonja have to think about what to do tonight. Should they watch a two-hour special on TV with their friends? Or should they study for an important math exam that they have to write tomorrow?**

You can help them out.

Activity 13C   Tough Decisions

As a class, try to solve Sonja and Lance's problem:

1. List as many choices as you can think of available to Sonja and Lance.

2. For each choice, write down its consequence — what would happen if they made that choice.

3. Decide which choice is best for Lance and Sonja.

4. Discuss why you made this decision.

Now to answer the main question for this section: What is a decision? A **decision** is a choice you make when you know the consequence or outcome of that choice.

HOW DO YOU MAKE DECISIONS?

In the activities in this chapter, you tried to make decisions. What is involved in making a decision? Here are four steps you can use to reach a decision.

> *Step One:*   Note the decision to be made.
> *Step Two:*   List the alternatives or possible choices.

Step Three: Consider the consequences, or possible outcomes or results, of each alternative.
Step Four: Make the decision.

How did Lance and Sonja make their decision? You have already tried to reach an answer for them. The next activity will help you reconsider your answers, using the four steps in the **decision-making process**.

Activity 13D   The Decision-Making Process

Lance and Sonja have to decide what to do tonight: to watch TV with their friends or study for an exam. Each box in this activity lists some alternatives. Your task is to provide the consequences for these alternatives. Then, you can decide which alternative would be the best. Do this activity on your own. You can discuss it in Activity 13E.

Example: They can choose to do neither. Possible consequences:
1. Both their friends and their math teacher will be angry with them.

2. They may be punished for not doing their work.

3. They will feel unhappy and angry because they accomplished nothing.

Is this a wise or unwise decision for Sonja and Lance to make?

Alternative 1: They can watch the TV special and study for their math test at the same time.
  List three possible consequences of this alternative.
  Is this a wise or unwise decision for Lance and Sonja?

Alternative 2: They can watch the TV special, and get to school early in the morning to study for their test.
  List three possible consequences or alternatives.
  Is this a wise or unwise decision for Lance and Sonja?

Alternative 3: They can watch the TV special and ask their teacher to give them a different math exam in two days' time.
  List three possible consequences of this alternative.
  Is this a wise or unwise decision for them?

Alternative 4: They could choose to watch the TV special only.
  List three possible consequences of this alternative.
  Is this a wise or unwise decision for them?

Alternative 5: They could stay home and study for the math exam and not watch the TV special with their friends.
List three possible consequences of this alternative.
Is this a wise or unwise decision?

Alternative 6: They could watch the TV special and pretend they are sick the next day.
List three possible consequences of this alternative.
Is this a wise or unwise decision?

Activity 13E   Talking About Decisions

When you finish Activity 13D, your class might hold a discussion to pool thoughts from all members of your class.

1. For each alternative, list several consequences suggested by class members.

2. Then, decide as a class upon the wisdom of each alternative.

3. Use this discussion to suggest other alternatives and their consequences.

4. Is there one best alternative to Sonja and Lance's problem?

Note: In decision making, there is not always a right or wrong alternative. You must make choices and each choice has its own *consequences*.

MORE DECISIONS

This section will give you some problems to think about. Remember, there are probably no right and wrong answers to these problems — there are only choices with their own consequences. To consider these problems, you will have to use the four steps in the *decision-making process*:

1. Note the decision to be made.

2. List the alternatives.

3. Consider the consequences.

4. Make the decision.

Here is an example of the way you might think about a problem so that you can make a good decision about it.

Example:

Monique is really excited. Five of her classmates have invited her to a pyjama party Friday evening. She has always wanted to be *in* with this group of girls. But, there's one catch. Her best friend, Patricia, wasn't invited. *What decision should Monique make about this invitation?*

Decision (to be made): Monique must decide whether or not to attend the pyjama party.

ALTERNATIVE	*CONSEQUENCE*
1. She could attend the party.	*If Patricia finds out she may be angry with Monique and feel she's been betrayed by her best friend.*
2. Monique could say "No, thank you."	*None of the girls may ask her to another party.*
3. She could go to the party and not tell Patricia and hope that Patricia wouldn't find out.	*Patricia might not find out, but Monique knows she will feel guilty.*
4. She could ask the girls to include Patricia.	*The girls may say "No," and Monique still has her problem.*
5. She could tell Patricia that she was going to the pyjama party and promise to tell her all about it.	*Patricia might be angry, but Monique knows she hasn't "gone behind her friend's back."*

Decision made: Because Patricia, her best friend, wasn't able to go with her, Monique decided to say, "No, thank you."

Activity 13F   Situations That Require Decisions

Here are some other situations that require decisions. Work in groups of three or four to reach your decisions.

1. **For each situation you should decide:**
   a) **the decision to be made**
   b) **the various alternatives or possibilities that could be chosen**
   c) **the consequences, or results, that could happen for each alternative**
   d) **the alternative which you believe makes the best decision**

Use the example for Monique's problem to help you set up this activity in your notebook.

Randy and Hubert are playing together at recess when they spot a wallet. They open it and find twenty dollars. There is no identification in the wallet. Hubert suggests they split the money and throw the wallet away. Randy says that they should give the wallet with the money in it to Mrs. Smithenson, the playground supervisor. Hubert calls Randy ''chicken'' and says that he won't play with Randy any more if they don't keep the money. In fact, he threatens to keep all of the money if Randy won't split it with him.

Suggest three alternatives and consequences for Randy. Which alternative do you think Randy should choose?

Ramone doesn't know what to do. He's done very poorly in English this year. In fact his English teacher has told him that he must pass tomorrow's English test or he'll fail. Jacques, however, has a solution. He had been kept in after school and, while the English teacher was out of the room, he stole a copy of tomorrow's test. Jacques was willing to share this copy with Ramone, and only Ramone. Nobody else would know. Suggest three alternatives and possible consequences for Ramone. Which alternative do you think Ramone should choose?

Lucille sits next to Harold. Harold has a terrible body odour. To put it bluntly, he stinks. In fact, his nickname is Stinky. Lucille complained at home to her mother about Harold. Her mother told her to tell her teacher. Lucille doesn't want to cause a problem either for herself or for Harold. Suggest three alternatives and consequences for Lucille. Which alternative do you think Lucille should choose?

Activity 13G   More Talk About Decisions

Your class might discuss each group's solutions to these problem situations. Use these questions to guide a class discussion:

1. How many different alternatives did the small groups suggest for each situation?

2. What are the consequences for each alternative?

3. Are there still other alternatives and consequences?

4. Is there an alternative or decision for each situation which all class members agree is the *best* one?

WRITING ABOUT DECISIONS

Use the drawing from *Whale Sound*, at the beginning of this chapter, to help with the brainstorming task set out in the following activity.

Activity 13H   Whale Thoughts

Look at the drawing on page 238.

1. In your notebook, write down as many words as you can think of about whales. Try for as many different words as you can.

2. Next, in your notebook, write for three minutes about the subject, whales. Don't stop your pen during the three minutes. If you can't think of anything to say, just keep writing *whales* on your page until you think of something new to say.

3. Your class might hold a talk session to share stories, thoughts, and ideas about whales.

With all of this thinking and talking about whales, you are now ready for your problem. Here it is!

> A group in your community has decided to build an arena large enough to hold three killer whales. The group will buy three whales and charge admission when people come to look at them. The profit from this project will be used to feed orphan children in poor countries.   →

The president of this group wants you to support the Whales in Our Community organization. What is your decision?

Here is your problem: *Provide the president with a written statement of your decision.* The final activity in this chapter will help you write your argument to support your decision.

Decisions Help to Write Sound Arguments

Activity 13I Thinking About Your Decision

You have already done some thinking about whales in Activity 13H. This task will help your focus upon your decision.

1. Write down the decision you have to make.

2. List as many choices as you can that support your decision.

3. List as many choices as you can that do not support your decision. (Hint: When you are making an argument, it is necessary to know both the facts which support your position and those which do not. This step will help you find out this kind of information.)

4. Consider the consequences for each choice or alternative in the above steps.

5. Look again at your statement in 1. Do you have enough points in your argument to support your decision? Or do you want to choose another decision?

   You will have to make up your mind before you go on to the next task: are you in favour of keeping whales in captivity in your community? Or do you oppose this idea?

Activity 13J Writing About Your Decision

Now you are ready to begin constructing the statement that you will deliver to the president of the Whales in Our Community organization. Use these steps to help you write your first draft.

1. For the first sentence in your paragraph, write out the decision that you made in the think-about step.

2. Choose the best choices that support your decision and write them as sentences in your paragraph. Usually you will have one sentence for each choice.

3. Start a new paragraph for those choices that do not support your decision.
   a) Write each choice as one sentence in this second paragraph.
   b) Follow each choice with an idea that shows why you do not agree with it.

4. Start another new paragraph that goes back to your decision.
   a) Write one or two sentences that repeat the decision you have made.
   b) Finish with the one most important argument you have to support your decision.

Activity 13K Rethinking Your Writing

It's probably best to do this activity with a writing partner.

1. Read your first paragraph to your partner.
   a) Your partner will listen to you and copy down, in note form, each argument you make.
   b) When you finish, discuss your partner's list:
      • Did he/she write down every point you made in your paragraph? If not, why? Is there a clearer way to make the points in your argument?
      • Talk about the order of the points in your argument: Is this the best order to make the points of your argument? If not, what is another possible way to arrange the points you make in your paragraph?

2. Read the second paragraph to your partner.
   a) Follow the same method as you did for the first paragraph.
   b) Check to make sure that you have provided a reason to support each point in this paragraph.

3. Look at your last paragraph.
   a) Does it restate the decision you have made?
   b) Does it add the one most important argument from the first paragraph to end your statement?
      Would, there be a better idea to place here?

4. Now, do the same thing for your reading partner. Go through steps 1 to 3 to help your partner think about what he or she has written.

Activity 13L   Writing Your Argument

1. Use your discussion with your writing partner to help you think about what you have written.

2. Remember, your partner has only offered you some suggestions. Take these suggestions as advice and make up your own mind.

3. Write the final draft of your argument.

Activity 13M   After You Write

You need an opportunity now to get someone to judge your argument as presented in your statement to the president of the Whales in Our Community group. Here are some ways in which you can get a response to your writing:

a) Form small groups in your class and read each other's statement. Decide among you the merits of each piece of writing and point out how each statement explains its owner's decision.

b) Ask another class in your school to read your arguments. Let them judge whether or not you presented a clear argument to support your decision.

c) Ask a committee of your parents to look at your writing. Get them to tell you whether or not your arguments support your decision.

Being Decisive

In this chapter you have learned to do two things: (1) to use four steps to help you in making decisions, and (2) to write an argument that puts forth your opinion — based upon your decision about a problem.

ENDINGS

It is almost the end of the year. Things are beginning to close down for the term. Librarians call in books; coaches stack away equipment.

It's time to collect memories of the year. What better way to do this than to leave a book of memories — your memories — for classes in the future to read.

Other people, living in other times, have left memories of their existence. This illustration contains some unique records of the past.

It displays some pictographs, or pictures, of rock paintings painted at various spots along the Churchill River system in northern Manitoba and Saskatchewan. These pictographs were painted years ago by Indian peoples.

T.E.H. Jones *The Aboriginal Rock Paintings of the Churchill River*

Activity 1

You are an archeologist, a person who studies artifacts, including paintings, from ancient civilizations. You have gone to visit the paintings in order to make a report on them.

1. As a class, talk about these questions:
   a) What do these rock paintings mean and why were they painted on the rocks beside a northern river?
   b) Of what value are these paintings to people living today?
   c) Should modern society do anything to preserve these paintings? Why?

2. Compare the paintings of these ancient Indians to this more recent art work. What are the similarities and the differences between the people who have drawn them?

3. Write a one- or two-paragraph report on the rock paintings of the Churchill River system.
   a) In your report, explain what these paintings are and what they mean.
   b) Include a comment on the value of these paintings for modern society.

Now you are ready to consider your own memories, your own record for future generations.

Activity 2

1. On your own, create a thought web with the words at the centre: *Our Class*. Let your thoughts run over the events of the past year:
   a) What were the highlights? the successes? the funny happenings?
   b) What were the difficult times? the failures? the sorrows? Include all of this in your thought web.

2. Choose the idea that most appeals to you from the thought web you created in 1. Write a paragraph to expand on this idea. Make it as interesting as you can. Someone may be reading it fifty years from now.

3. Your teacher will then form an *editorial team* — a group of three or four students to choose the selections:
   a) The editorial team should read all of the paragraphs produced for this activity.
   b) The team must select at least one contribution from each student in the class.
   c) The editorial team then returns the chosen paragraphs to their authors.

4. Each student reads his or her chosen paragraph.
   a) Revise the paragraph by adding one additional detail to improve your memory.
   b) Revise the paragraph by subtracting something that is not important.
   c) Reread the paragraph an additional time to see if there are some details that could be added to the paragraph to give a more complete record of the event described.

5. Your teacher will select a *design team* to decide how to reproduce this book of memories:
   a) How will these paragraphs be reproduced? Should you make only one copy or produce one for each member of the class?
   b) How will they be arranged in the book?
   c) Can pictures be included and reproduced?
   d) Is there some art work that could be included?
   e) What kind of binding should the book have?
   f) What is a good cover design?

6. Your teacher will also select a *proofreading team*.
   a) Each student should give his or her revised paragraph to this team.
   b) The team will read the paragraph one last time to look for mechanical errors: punctuation, spelling, sentence structure.

7. Now the paragraphs should be returned to the editorial team. This team will make the final selection and arrangement of all of the material to be included in the book of memories.

8. The editorial team will give the final manuscript to the *design and production team*, who will be responsible for the final production.

Happy memories and good communicating.

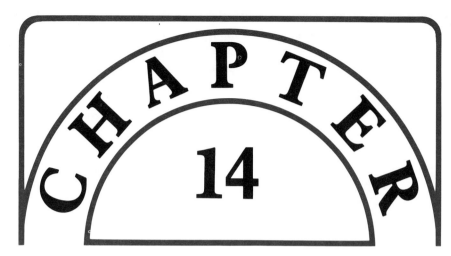

CHAPTER 14

RESOURCE CHAPTER
GRAMMAR

BUILDING GRAMMAR CONCEPTS

It's easy to see that language is made up of words. Big words, small words, hard words, easy words — they are the building blocks upon which much of your communication is based.

Words fit together in interesting ways. This chapter is all about the ways words work together, about how they fit into a system. This system is called a **grammar**. A grammar is a scientific system that shows how words work together so that they communicate meaning.

Looking at Nouns, Verbs, and Sentences

This next series of activities is about **sentences** and **nouns** and **verbs**. When you finish these activities you should know what each term means and be able to write sentences and recognize the nouns and verbs in your sentences.

Activity 14A   Noun or Verb: How Can You Tell?

1. Write the letters of your first name vertically, as James has done:

2. Use each letter in your name as the first letter of a word that suggests some action or motion. James would write something like this:

3. Next, think of some person or thing or place that could do the actions suggested by the words in your list:

   James's examples: Horses *jump*.
   Mosquitoes *annoy*.
   Rivers *meet*.
   Insurance adjusters *estimate*.
   Canaries *swing*.

Review: Nouns and Verbs

Words like *horses* and *mosquitoes* are called NOUNS. They provide the name of a person, a place, or a thing. Words like *jump* and *annoy* are called VERBS. These words suggest action or movement.

You may want to look in a dictionary to find out about some words. They will be marked as *n.* or *v.* Here is an example of what you may see:
        goad 1. *n.* [*for noun*] long stick for driv-
      ing cattle. 2. *v.* [*for verb*] to drive with,
      prod, incite.

---

4. Next, apply the definitions of noun and verb to the sentences you created in 3.

Activity 14B   Building Sentences

In Activity 14A you wrote short sentences of two or three words. Let's see if you can build on these sentence stubs, to add more information to your ideas.

James, from Activity 14A, might write sentences that look something like this:

- The frightened horses jumped the wire fence.
- The pesky mosquitoes, which came from the swamp, annoyed the grazing buffalo.
- The rivers meet at the forks, which are about forty miles east of town.
- The insurance adjuster estimated the flood damage in our basement.
- The yellow canaries swing from their perch in the golden cage, keeping me awake all night.

1. Try expanding the sentence stubs that James created: horses jump, mosquitoes annoy, rivers meet, insurance adjusters estimate, canaries swing.

2. Next, take the sentence stubs you created for Activity 14A. Expand these sentences to make them more interesting by adding words to them.

3. Write your answers in your notebook.

The main noun in a sentence is called the **subject.** The main verb is called the **predicate.** The noun and the verb in a sentence are always connected. In the following sentence, the subject and predicate do not go together. They are not connected.

> S   P
> The *river/melted* in the frying pan.

A more logical sentence that begins with *The river* would be

> S   P
> The *river/meandered* across the field and out of sight.

and a more logical sentence containing the predicate *melted* would be

> S   P
> The *butter* for the popcorn/*melted* in the frying pan.

Now it's time for you to try your hand at writing subjects and predicates that are connected.

Activity 14C   Subject + Predicate = Sentence

1. Rewrite each of the following sentences as two complete sentences.

2. Give each subject a proper predicate, and each predicate a proper subject.

   a) The *newspaper/gave* the woman the incorrect change.
   b) The *skidoo/waved* to the madly cheering crowd.
   c) The *gas station/modelled* the latest in male fashion.
   d) The *street light/bowed* to the applause of the audience.
   e) The *cartoon/walked* slowly through the art gallery.

It is possible to place more labels on sentences.
- The subject and all the words which go with it are called the **complete subject**. The main noun in a complete subject is called the **simple subject**. Here are some examples:

> simple subject
>
> The happy *cheers* of the winning team echoed throughout the school.
> complete subject

> simple subject
>
> The quiet *swish* of the canoe barely disturbed the sleeping lake.
> complete subject

- The predicate and all of the words which go with it are called the **complete predicate**. The main verb within a complete predicate is called a **simple predicate**. Here are some examples:

> simple predicate
>
> The cyclist *raced* quickly around the curve and out of sight.
> complete predicate

> simple predicate
>
> The horse *kicked* her heels in the air.
> complete predicate

Let's see what you can do with subjects and predicates.

Activity 14D   Complete Subjects and Complete Predicates

1. Add words to these sentences to expand the complete subject:
   a) *The high jumper*/cleared the bar with ease.
   b) *The wind*/played a big factor in the game.
   c) *The marathon runner*/staggered into the stadium.
   d) *The crowd*/cheered its support.

2. Add words to these sentences to expand the complete predicate:
   a) The radio/*blared.*
   b) The dj/*played the record.*
   c) The song/*made the top 40 list.*
   d) The announcer/*interrupted the program.*

3. Add a complete predicate of your own to these subject starters:

complete subject	*complete predicate*
a) The drummer in green cords/	. . . .
b) The music from the organ/	. . . .
c) The guitar in her hands/	. . . .
d) The singer/	. . . .

4. Add a complete subject of your own to these predicates:

complete subject	*complete predicate*
a) . . . ./	read a story to the young children.
b) . . . ./	sang a quiet lullaby.
c) . . . ./	strummed a folk tune on his guitar.
d) . . . ./	beat time with her drum stick.

Origami is the Japanese art form of folding paper to represent flowers, birds, or other things. The paper-folding task in the next activity will help you review nouns and verbs.

Activity 14E   Noun and Verb Origami

1. Find an ordinary piece of paper. Any kind will do, and it can be any colour.

2. Make something out of this paper—such as a ball, a boa constrictor, a horse, a castle, anything.

3. Here is your challenge. You can't write on this paper — no pen, pencil, lipstick, crayon, or blood.

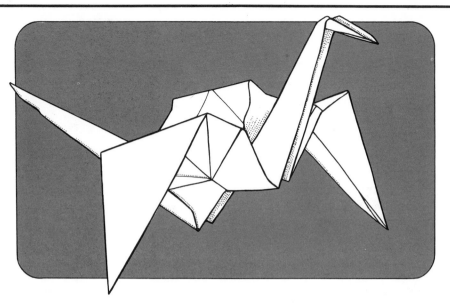

4. You may rip it, bite it, chew it, stamp on it, crumple it, fold it, twist it. But you can't write or draw on it.

5. When you have finished your paper folding, choose a noun or a verb title for your masterpiece.

6. Write your title on a piece of paper as neatly as you can.

7. Staple your creation and title to a bulletin board to make a class display of interesting art work, as well as a review of nouns and verbs.

Some words can be used as a noun or a verb. They can be a noun in one sentence and a verb in another. Let's look at the word *corral* to see what this means.

In this sentence, *corral* is used as a noun:

The *corral* held the wild horses.

In this one, *corral* is used as a verb:

The sheriff *corralled* the bank robbers in the canyon.

Here is another example, using the word *band*:

As a noun: The *band* played at the opening ceremonies.
As a verb: The musk ox *band* together for protection.

Activity 14F   Noun = Verb

1. In your notebook, write two sentences for each of the following words. The first sentence should use the word as a noun, and the second as a verb:

   a) water
   b) fish
   c) stalk

   d) fence
   e) box
   f) book

2. Make up a list of your own words which can be used as either a noun or a verb. You should be able to find at least ten words.

Activity 14G   Nouns and Sentences Again

1. Write your name vertically, as shown in the example, and use each letter in your name as one letter in a noun that tells what you do or who you are.

Examples:

Diphak might write —   Yvonne might write —
    ban **D** member   **Y** WCA swimming instructor
      p **I** tcher   **V** aledictorian
       P ercussionist   Newf **O** undlander
   brot **H** er   co **N** tralto
    go **A** lie   blo **N** de
     s **K** ier   daught **E** r

2. Write a sentence in which the first letter of each word spells your last or surname. The words must occur in sequence.

   Example: Someone with the surname *Zerebeski* might write:
   Zebras eat radishes easily before elephants sip Kool-aid intently.

   a) As a class, try to compose a sentence for the surname Zerebeski.
   b) Then tackle your own name.

Some nouns always begin with a capital letter, even when they occur in the middle of a sentence. Others sometimes begin with a capital letter, and sometimes not. Look at the examples in Activity 14G. The word *Newfoundlander* starts with a capital letter; the word daughter does not. Why is this so? Read the following explanation.

Common Nouns and Proper Nouns

Nouns that name a special person or place or thing are capitalized. They are called **proper nouns**. Proper nouns like these are capitalized: Fido; Orillia, Ontario; Princess Diana; Queen Elizabeth Highway. All other nouns are not capitalized, unless they are at the beginning of a sentence. They are called **common nouns**. Common nouns like these are not capitalized: dog, city, province, princess, road.

Activity 14H   Common and Proper Nouns

1. **Form groups of five or six students.**

2. **Share the sentences which you wrote about your surname in the last activity.**

3. **Check to make certain that you have capitalized all proper nouns and not capitalized any common nouns, unless they are at the beginning of a sentence.**

Looking at Adjectives

Read these paragraphs and think about the italicized words. What do they have in common?

The mate had no idea that Andrew was not quite sixteen. Almost no one would have guessed that, for he was tall, with a *confident* face and *broad* shoulders and a *narrow-hipped* way of walking that made him seem much older than *his* years. Andrew had *brown curly* hair, not long, not really short, and a *strong straight* nose, *gray* eyes and *even* teeth. There was something about *his large* hands and the set of his neck that made people believe he was *strong* and *capable*.

James Houston, *River Runners*

Among the contestants [at the William's Lake Rodeo in British Columbia] are the *Indian* children, who with *their natural* ability, seem equally at home in the saddle or riding bareback. They . . . are proud of *their* horses and *their own Western-style* clothing; the *faded* levis, the *colourful* shirts, and the *broad-brimmed* hats which everyone wears, even the people who have just come to look, and who have never been on a horse in their lives.

Mae Worth, ''Little Britches Rodeo''

The answer is this: all of these words describe nouns. That is, they tell more about nouns. This chart shows you this connection.

Noun	*Adjective*
face	confident
shoulders	broad
hair	brown curly
clothing	Western-style
levis	faded

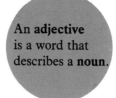

An **adjective** is a word that describes a **noun**.

Activity 14I   Noun + Adjective

1. **Reread the two paragraphs.**

2. **Then, complete the list of nouns and adjectives that was started in the explanation.**

3. **Remember to draw an arrow from the adjective to the noun it describes. This will remind you that adjectives are words that describe nouns.**

The word *modify* is a **synonym** for (or another word for) *describe.* So another definition for an adjective is this: An adjective is a word that modifies a noun.

Activity 14J   Adjective Pictures

1. **Look at these adjective designs:**

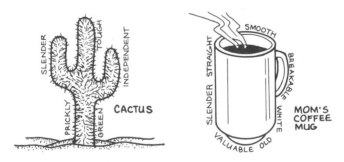

2. **In your notebook, sketch five simple objects, such as a guitar, a chair, an elephant, and a car. Don't spend too much time with your drawing.**

3. **Decorate your outline with adjectives. Use a dictionary or a thesaurus to help you.**

4. Choose your best sketch and redraw it on a separate piece of paper.

5. Use the sketches to make a class display of adjectives.

Activity 14K   An Adjective Story Book

1. Choose a book or a short story you have read recently.

2. Skim this book to look for adjectives.

3. List in your notebook six adjectives and the nouns they describe or modify.

4. Illustrate your word choices in a booklet. Save these booklets for a display for parents' day, or some other special occasion in your classroom.

Example:

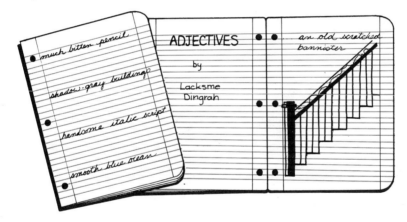

Activity 14L   More Adjectives

1. List the following nouns in your notebook.

2. After each noun write two adjectives that could describe it.
   a) car
   b) horse
   c) tree
   d) cloud
   e) music
   f) cat

3. Then, write each noun and one of the adjectives in a complete sentence. Make your sentences at least eight words in length.

Activity 14M   From Adjective to Paragraph

This painting was done by Tom Thomson.

Pine Island, Georgian Bay Tom Thomson

1. As a class, brainstorm a list of adjectives to describe this scene.

2. In your notebook, write a paragraph about the scene, using adjectives from your list.

3. Underline each adjective you use in this paragraph.

Looking at Adverbs

You have already learned to identify verbs in sentences. Verbs tell you what action or movement is occurring in a sentence: The cowboy *rode* the wild bull.

You can add words to sentences to give more information about the verb, to describe more completely exactly what action has occurred. Look at this example:

The cowboy *rode* the wild bull.

> easily
> skillfully
> yesterday
> fearfully

Words that describe, or modify, verbs are called **adverbs**. Adverbs give specific information about *when, where,* or *how* an action happens.

Examples:
Tom drove home.   When ? . . . . today.

  adverb
Tom drove home *today.*

WHEN

The band marched.   Where? . . . . outside.

  adverb
The band marched *outside.*

WHERE

Ingrid looked for a clue to the crime.   How ? . . . . carefully.

  adverb
Ingrid looked *carefully* for a clue to the crime.

HOW

Activity 14N   Adverbs = When/Where/How

1. **Read through this list of adverbs and decide whether each could answer the question *when, where,* or *how*:**

   a) **nightly**   c) **there**
   b) **away**   d) **anywhere**

e) quickly
f) tomorrow
g) early

h) sometimes
i) calmly
j) soon

2. In your notebook, write each of these adverbs in a sentence of at least eight words in length. Underline each adverb.

3. Divide into pairs.

4. Read the sentences that your partner has written, and rewrite them in your partner's notebook. This time, place the adverb in a different position in the sentence.

   Example:

   first sentence: Mom, I'll take the garbage out *tomorrow.*

   partner's change: Mom, *tomorrow* I'll take the garbage out.

5. As a class, discuss this question: Does this change in the position of the adverb make a change in the meaning of the sentence?

Activity 140   The Best Adverb

1. Rewrite each sentence in your notebook and supply the missing adverbs. Use your dictionary or thesaurus to find the best adverb possible for each blank.
   a) Pick up the package _____ and open it _____ .
   b) Gretchen _____ slammed the door and walked _____ into the middle of the crowd.
   c) The sea rippled _____ as the moon shone _____ in the night sky.

An old word game involves making up *Tom Swifties.* A Tom Swifty matches an adverb with the main part of the sentence to create a word joke:

"I hate winter," said Tom *coldly.*
"I hate seafood," said Tom *crabbily.*
"I love Christmas," said Tom *merrily.*
"I like presents," said Tom *openly.*
"Take my knife," Tom said *sharply* and *pointedly.*
"Don't touch that button," Tom said *pressingly.*

Activity 14P   Tom Swifties

1. Try making some Tom Swifties.

2. "Why not have a Tom Swifty Contest?" Tom said *competitively.*

Looking at Prepositions

Prepositions act as direction markers in sentences. They show how nouns can connect to other parts of a sentence. The group of words that go with a preposition is called a **prepositional phrase**.

Here are some examples of prepositions and prepositional phrases used in sentences:

```
                  preposition
                       |
    The goat in the field chased the hobo.
                  prepositional phrase


                          preposition
                               |
    The pelican flew slowly over the river.
                          prepositional phrase


            preposition   preposition
                 |             |
    The eagle flew to the edge of the cliff.
            prepositional phrase   prepositional phrase
```

Activity 14Q   Prepositions

1. Use one of the prepositions in the box on the following page to construct a sentence to describe each of these pictures.

   Example:

   a) The book *on the chair* is   b)
      my history text.

c)   d)   e)

| Prepositions |
| on |
| beside |
| between |
| behind |
| under |

Activity 14R   Prepositional Phrases

1. Using the prepositional phrase that is written beneath each picture, construct a sentence to describe the action in the picture.

2. Write your sentences in your notebook.

a)

at the store

b)

towards the dog

c)

off the table

d)

by the brook

e)

among the pigeons

f)

underneath the tree

g)

across the ocean

h)

against the rock

i)

beyond the horizon

j)

during recess

Activity 14S More Prepositions

1. Write sentences that contain each of these prepositional phrases:
   a) aboard the ship
   b) after the game
   c) beside the horse
   d) to the farm
   e) down the well
   f) about his business
   g) along the trail
   h) without a complaint
   i) through the canyon
   j) by the church yard

Activity 14T Prepositional Phrases in a Short Story

This paragraph comes from "On Nimpish Lake," written by the Canadian writer Ethel Wilson.

1. Read the paragraph over once, looking for prepositions and prepositional phrases.

2. List the prepositional phrases in your notebook.

Sandhill cranes fly high over Nimpish Lake. Geese fly high too. They fly south from the vast northlands beyond the Arctic watershed. They fly strongly, with outstretched necks. Their heads are thrust forward. Their voices are raised in harsh and musical clamour. Why do they cry, cry, cry, as they fly. Is it jubilation or argument or part of the business of flying. Who knows how much they see of the forests of British Columbia as they fly south. How much do they see of the mountains and valleys in their spearhead flight, and how much do they see of human habitation. Their old leader seeks a lake that he knows, or a chain of lakes, where they will camp for the night. They will circle down when the wise old leader sees his lake. They will circle down talking their vehement goose talk. There they will rest where they are safe in protected places, or where they are remote from men. Perhaps they will stay for a few days. Some of these strong geese are tired. The wise old leader knows.

Ethel Wilson, "On Nimpish Lake"

3. From your list of prepositional phrases in Ethel Wilson's paragraph, select the six you like best.

4. Use these phrases in your own sentences. Each sentence should be at least ten words long.

Looking at Verbs Again

This description comes from *Gold-Fever Trail: A Klondike Adventure* by Canadian writer Monica Hughes.

The paragraph is written in the past tense. That is, it describes the action by telling you that everything has already happened. The story is being reported to you after it is finished.

> At that moment the wind *tore* the grey clouds apart and through the opening the sun *shone* on the dazzling emerald green of Crater Lake below them. Ahead among the tumble of foothills and mountains *was* the glint of other lakes, and there, far in the distance, they *could see* a silver thread winding away to the Northwest. It *was* the Yukon River!
>
> Monica Hughes, *Gold-Fever Trail: A Klondike Adventure*

Activity 14U   Past Tense to Present Tense

1. Rewrite this passage from Monica Hughes's novel in your notebook.

2. Change each of the italicized verbs from the past tense to the present tense.

   Example:
   past tense: I *saw* the mountains in the distance.
   present tense: I *see* the mountains in the distance.

Activity 14V   The Verb "to eat"

1. On your own, find as many verbs as possible that mean *to eat* and list them in your notebook.

2. Using these verbs to help you, write a paragraph of at least eight sentences to describe lunchtime in your school or some other place where people gather to eat.

3. Change paragraphs with a writing partner and rewrite this paragraph in your partner's book, using the opposite tense. That is, if your partner wrote the paragraph in the past tense, rewrite it in the present tense, and vice versa.

An Overview

This section contains two quizzes to help you review and think about some of the grammar concepts introduced in this chapter.

Activity 14W   Quiz 1

Discuss the answers to these questions in class.

1. Which sentence would you use if you wanted to make sure that you were not making a mistake in English?
   a) I ain't got my homework done.
   b) I haven't done my homework.

2. Which sentence tells you that the race happens every week?
   a) He ran the race Wednesday.
   b) He runs the race Wednesdays.

3. Which sentence is an example of *nonstandard usage?*
   a) I drunk my coke before leaving.
   b) I drank my coke before leaving.

4. Which sentence tells you that the action will happen in the future?
   a) I will go with you.
   b) I went with you.

5. Which sentence is written in the *negative form*?
   a) I ran to school, but I was late.
   b) I didn't run to school, and I was late.

6. Which sentence is an example of the *double negative form*?
   a) I don't have anything to do.
   b) I don't have nothing to do.

7. Which sentence contains several *descriptive adjectives*?
   a) Our hockey rink is cold, dusty, and barnish.
   b) Our hockey rink is suitable for many purposes.

8. Which sentence tells you that the team worked well together?
   a) The team worked hard to get the ball over the centre line.
   b) The team worked with Swiss-watch precision.

9. Which of the following is an example of a *sentence fragment*?
   a) As the goalie reached for the puck, it took a wild carom into the slot.
   b) The centre found himself eyeing the goalie. Corner pocket!

10. Which sentence contains a *simile?*
    a) She took a huge swipe with her racquet, like an eagle swooping on its prey.
    b) She hit the ball solidly, and sent it swiftly and accurately over the net, totally confusing her opponent.

Activity 14X   Quiz 2

Rewrite these sentences in your notebook, following the directions.

1. **Write this sentence in the present tense:**
   Anne of Green Gables **was a favourite book among many Canadian young people.**

2. **Change** *the book's author* **to a prepositional phrase beginning with** *of.*
   The book's author is L.M. Montgomery.

3. **Change the verb in this sentence to the past tense.**
   The story occurs on a farm near Cavendish, Prince Edward Island.

4. **Find a synonym for the noun** *book.*
   The book has been adapted as a musical.

5. **Change the verb phrase in this sentence to the future tense.**
   The musical version has enchanted thousands of visitors at the Charlottetown Summer Festival.

6. **Change the verb in this sentence to the past tense.**
   The heroine in the story is Anne Shirley.

7. **Rewrite this sentence so that it begins with** *Marilla and Matthew Cuthbert.*
   Anne Shirley is adopted by Marilla and Matthew Cuthbert.

8. **Rewrite this sentence, placing the adverb** *quickly* **in a different position within the sentence.**
   Anne quickly wins the heart of Matthew.

9. **Add the adjective** *stern* **to this sentence so that it describes Marilla.**
   Marilla has to cope with Anne's wild imagination.

10. **Rewrite this sentence beginning with** *Mark Twain said that Anne . . .*
    Mark Twain said, "Anne is the sweetest creation of child life yet written."

Wrap-Up

Like Peppermint Patty, you have been conceptualizing in this chapter. You have been finding out about grammar. By now you should know several concepts fairly well: sentence, noun, verb, adjective, adverb, preposition, prepositional phrase.

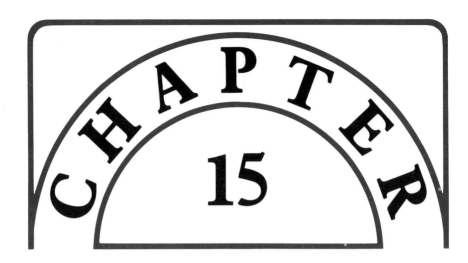

CHAPTER 15

RESOURCE CHAPTER
SENTENCE COMBINING

LANGUAGE BUILDING BLOCKS: SENTENCE COMBINING

The whole of anything is made up of its parts. Let's think about it. A jigsaw is made up of its pieces. Your school is made up of its students and teachers. Canada is made up of its provinces and territories. The Toronto Maple Leafs is made up of its team players or the Atlantic Symphony is made up of its musicians.

Language is like this too. The whole is made up of its parts. In the last chapter you studied the parts of a sentence: noun, verb, adjective, adverb, preposition. This chapter will look further at the parts of a sentence. In this chapter, you will learn not only what the parts are, but more important, how to use them. All of the sentence-combining activities in this chapter have been designed to give you the ability to control the parts that make up sentences.

Coordinating Conjunctions: *And* and *But*

Do you remember sentences like these from your beginning readers?

Spot ran to the door.
Muff ran to the door.

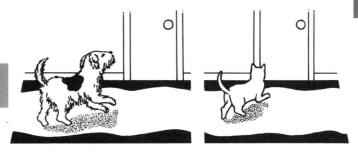

In later grades, you learned to write these two sentences as one sentence, like this.

Spot and Muff ran to the door.

This last example takes fewer words to give the same message. The first example requires ten words; the second example, seven. For most writing tasks, the second example is a better sentence. It gives the message more directly and with fewer words.

The first example, however, might be used to give a definite feeling — one of excitement and action. Try reading the two examples aloud to see which one can be made to sound faster and most exciting. In these sentences, the nouns are combined to make them shorter. Verbs can also be combined in sentences. Here is an example:

Spot found his dish.
Spot ate his supper.
(combine . . . and)

The directions tell you to combine these two base sentences with the word *and*, like this:

Rewrite: Spot found his dish and ate his supper.

Activity 15A Combining Nouns . . . Combining Verbs

1. Combine each set of basic sentences to make one sentence, following the sentence-combining directions:
   a) Lois Marshall is a Canadian operatic star.
      Jon Vickers is a Canadian operatic star
         (combine nouns . . . and)

   b) Barbara Ann Scott won an Olympic gold medal in figure skating.
      Karen Magnusson won an Olympic gold medal in figure skating.
         (combine nouns . . . and)

   c) Margaret Laurence is a Canadian novelist.
      Hugh MacLennan is a Canadian novelist.
         (combine nouns . . . and)

   d) The detective rang the door bell.
      The detective delivered a subpoena.
         (combine verbs . . . and)

   e) The villain looked at the detective.
      The villain reached into her pocket.
         (combine verbs . . . and)

   f) The detective trembled with fear.
      The detective ran down the road.
         (combine verbs . . . and)

In Activity 15A you practised combining two sentences by joining nouns or verbs. You can use this skill in your own writing. To do so, you have to make two choices:
   1. to leave your writing as two sentences
   2. to combine your basic sentences into one sentence
For what reason, you might ask, should you combine sentences? Well, for one thing, the length of sentences has an influence upon the meaning they suggest.

Here is an example of the way length suggests meaning. Longer sentences seem to give a feeling of quietness and smoothness, or they can be used to build quietly toward something big, something exciting —to a climax. Shorter sentences seem to give a feeling of quickness and excitement.

In this paragraph from "How the Human People Got the First Fire," George Clutesi sets the scene for his story with long, quiet, and serious sentences:

> So the great chiefs from all the land would command that all men come forward and try to capture the fire. The strongest would boast that he would go forth to the land of the Wolf people and force his way into the village and bring the fire back.

But no hunter could capture the fire from the Wolf people. The author stresses this problem by using short, fast-moving sentences:

> No one spoke. No one moved. All eyes were cast down. All had tried and had failed. All the people were very sad indeed.
> George Clutesi, "How the Human People Got the First Fire"

Activity 15B   To Combine or Not to Combine

For each of the following sets of sentences, you must decide whether or not to combine the sentences in the set. To make this decision, look at the purpose for each sentence: Does the situation require short or long sentences?

1. Make your decision and write your answer in your notebook.

2. As a class, discuss your answers: Why did you make your choice?
   Example:
   The centre reached for the puck.
   He cradled it on the blade of his stick. (combine . . . ?)
   purpose: *to create action and excitement*
   Rewrite: The centre reached for the puck. He cradled it on the blade of his stick.
   These sentences were not joined. The two shorter sentences give a feeling of action.

   a) The puck whistled from the edge of his blade.
      The goalie's leg shot out, automatically.   (combine . . . ?)
         purpose: *to stress the quick movement and skill of the goalie*
   b) Zuck felt the boards ram against his shoulder.
      He heard a strange, grinding noise.   (combine . . . ?)
         purpose: *to create the feeling of time passing slowly*

c) The crowd rose to its feet.
   It made no sound.
   It looked at Zuck with pity. (combine . . . ?)
   > purpose: *to stress the quietness in the hockey arena*

d) Klein shot the puck to the blueline.
   It did not go over.
   Glor slapped at it.
   He missed. (combine . . . ?)
   > purpose: *to show rapid action*

e) The referee sent Robertson to the penalty box.
   The crowd roared its approval. (combine . . . ?)
   > purpose: *to begin to build the excitement*

f) Petrie shot the puck.
   It hit the goal post.
   Mackie fired again.
   The puck disappeared in a tangle of legs.
   The red light flashed on. (combine . . . ?)
   > purpose: *to build up to a climax*

g) The players walked over the wood floor to the dressing room.
   They sat down on the plank bench.
   They sat in silence.
   They looked straight ahead.
   They had lost the final game. (combine . . . ?)
   > purpose: *to show sadness and dejection*

Activity 15C Looking for Sentence Combinations

1. Look at the sentences in one of the stories you are reading in language arts class. Find four examples of sentences that
   - are short to stress action or to emphasize an idea
   - are long to stress quietness and easiness

2. Copy a short paragraph from a story you have been reading into your notebook. Write comments at the side of it to explain the author's use of sentence length.

Example:

short sentence to state a fact →

By midafternoon the river was changing. It was no longer simply smooth and black and silent. It started to develop "fish eyes," small whirlpools caused by the rush of water, and "hay stacks" where white water thundered angrily against hidden rocks. Far to the north they heard a deep-throated roar.

long sentence which causes the pace to slow down, creating suspense
It begins to build toward a climax.

short sentence to mark the threat of the waterfall

James Houston, *River Runners*

3. Examine a paragraph that you wrote sometime in the past. Recopy it into your notebook. Show how you did, or did not, use sentence length to echo the action in your writing.

In the last activities, you practised combining sentences. You most likely used *and* to join many of the sentences. This section looks at how you use *and* and *but* more definitely so that you will know exactly what they mean.

Review
You know how to combine these sentences:
Alberta joined Confederation in 1905.
Newfoundland joined in 1949.   (combine . . . and)
Rewrite: Alberta joined Confederation in 1905, and Newfoundland joined in 1949.

What happens if you join these sentences with the word *but?*
Alberta joined Confederation in 1905, but Newfoundland joined in 1949.

Explanation
a) *And* is used to add information, like a sign in mathematics.
   Example: The dog is black.
          The cat is white.   (combine . . ., and)
          Rewrite: The dog is black, and the cat is white.
b) *But* is used to contrast things, to show how things are different, almost like a sign in mathematics.
   Example: The dog is black.
          The cat is white.   (combine . . ., but)
          Rewrite: The dog is black, but the cat is white.

Activity 15D   And . . . or . . . But

1. Solve these sentence-combining problems by choosing *and* or *but* to combine each set of sentences.
   a) Farming is a major activity on the Prairies.
      Fishing occurs in the Maritime provinces.   (combine . . .?)
      purpose: *to add information*
   b) English is the dominant language of Ontario.
      French is the main language of Quebec.   (combine . . .?)
      purpose: *to show a contrast between these provinces*

c) Prairie winters can be severe.
Winters on the Pacific coast are usually mild.　　(combine . . . ?)
purpose: *to stress the differences between the two regions*

2. Read each set of sentences and decide whether they contrast information or add information. Rewrite these sentences in your notebook, using *and* or *but* to combine them. Be prepared to defend your choices in class.
Hint: Some clues are hidden within the sentences, usually the second sentence.

a) Oil is produced in Alberta.
Little oil is found in Ontario.　　(combine . . . ?)

b) Sir John A. Macdonald was Canada's Prime Minister.
Alexander Mackenzie was Canada's second Prime Minister.
　　(combine . . . ?)

c) The Inuit inhabit the Arctic region of Canada.
The Cree Indians live in the region just south of the tundra.
　　(combine . . . ?)

d) Very little snow falls on the North Pole because the air is so dry.
The Maritime region and Newfoundland receive heavy snowfall.　　(combine . . . ?)

e) During the American Civil War, many Black people used the Underground Railway to escape to Canada.
Some Black Canadians living today are descendants of these escaped slaves.　　(combine . . . ?)

f) New Brunswick was part of Nova Scotia until 1784.
It was known as Sunbury Country.　　(combine . . . ?)

g) The flag of Nova Scotia was the first flag among Canada's provinces.
It was also the first flag among all Britain's colonies.
　　(combine . . . ?)

Looking at Maria Campbell's Writing

Maria Campbell, a contemporary Canadian writer, wrote her autobiography (or story of her life). Called *Halfbreed*, it tells the story of her as a Métis girl growing up in northern Saskatchewan. It is a moving account of the joys and sorrows of a group of people who had to struggle for their recognition in Canadian society. *Halfbreed* is one of the first of a number of books written by Native People who are telling Canadian society about their point of view.

> The immigrants who came and homesteaded the land were predominantly Germans and Swedes. On small farms they raised pigs, poultry, a few cows and a bit of grain. I remember these people so well, for I thought they must be the richest and most beautiful on earth. They could buy pretty cloth for dresses, ate apples and oranges, and they had toothbrushes and brushed their teeth every day. I was afraid of them. They looked cold and frightening, and seldom smiled, unlike my own people who laughed, cried, danced, and fought and shared everything. These people rarely raised their voices, and never shared with each other, borrowing or buying instead. They didn't understand us, just shook their heads and thanked God they were different.
>
> Maria Campbell, *Halfbreed*

Let's look more closely at Maria Campbell's writing as an example of sentence combining.

Example 1:
   The immigrants came.
   The immigrants homesteaded the land   (combine . . . and)
   Rewrite: *The immigrants came and homesteaded the land.*
The rules for combining these sentences are:
   a) Join the second sentence to the first with *and*.
   b) Delete the words in the second sentence that are marked with an X.

Example 2:
   The immigrants raised pigs.
   They raised poultry.   (combine . . .,)
   They raised a few cows.   (combine . . .,)
   They raised a bit of grain.   (combine . . . and)
   Rewrite: *The immigrants raised pigs, poultry, a few cows and a bit of grain.*

Activity 15E   Looking at Maria Campbell's Writing

Combine these sets of sentences. Remember that this symbol **X** means delete or leave out the words marked. Write your answers in your notebook.

1. The immigrants looked cold.
   T~~h~~ey lo~~o~~ked frightening.   (combine . . . and)
   T~~h~~ey seldom smiled.   (combine . . ., and)

2. My people laughed.
   M~~y~~ pe~~o~~ple cried.   (combine . . .,)
   M~~y~~ pe~~o~~ple danced.   (combine . . .,)
   M~~y~~ pe~~o~~ple fought.   (combine . . ., and)
   M~~y~~ pe~~o~~ple shared everything.   (combine . . . and)

3. The immigrants could buy pretty cloth for dresses.
   T~~h~~ey ate apples.   (combine . . .,)
   T~~h~~ey a~~t~~e oranges.   (combine . . . and)
   They had toothbrushes.   (combine . . ., and)
   T~~h~~ey brushed their teeth every day.   (combine . . . and)

4. They didn't understand us.
   T~~h~~ey just shook their heads.   (combine . . .,)
   T~~h~~ey thanked God they were different.   (combine . . . and)

Labels and Names

In these activities, you have been working with parts of sentences. These parts have names. This chart shows you the names that are given to all of the structures you have been working with.

Example 1:

Two nouns that are joined with *and* are called **compound nouns**. *And* is called a **conjunction**.

      conjunction
        |
Ballet and jazz are two dance forms.
└──┬──┘
compound nouns

              conjunction
                 |
Our family went to the zoo and the planetarium.
              └───┬───┘
             compound nouns

Example 2:
Two verbs that are joined by *and* are called **compound verbs**.

conjunction
|
The leader jumped and shouted when the team won.
compound verbs

conjunction
|
The pilot turned and dove to the right to miss the tower.
compound verbs

Example 3:
Two sentences that are joined by *and*, *but*, or *or* are called **compound sentences.**

conjunction

sentence #1 | sentence #2

The band stood up on the stage and the trumpet player played her encore.

conjunction

sentence #1 | sentence #2

The buffalo returned to its grazing, and the wolf crept slowly on.

conjunction

sentence #1 | sentence #2

The ancient statue fell to the floor, but it did not break.

Note: Compound sentences are often joined with a comma (,) along with the conjunction. Some writers may omit this comma.

Example:
The typist sat at the computer, and it began to beep.
or
The typist sat at the computer and it began to beep.

Activity 15F   Compound Everything

1. **From the following list of nouns, construct three sentences that contain compound nouns.**

2. **From the list of verbs, construct three sentences that contain compound verbs.**

3. From the lists of nouns and verbs, construct two sentences that contain both compound nouns and compound verbs.

4. From the sentences you have constructed for 1, 2, and 3, construct one compound sentence.

Nouns	*Verbs*
fish	to roar
flashlight	to bow
prize	to fall
game	to carry
clock	to fly
antelope	to whistle
salmon	to bend
river	to squeak
Antarctic Circle	to think
space suit	to freeze
robot	to talk
mission control	to orbit

Subordinate Conjunctions and Clauses

This section takes you deeper into the mysteries of the structures or parts of sentences and of sentence combining.

What does this sentence mean?

The wind blew *and* the branch broke.

Did the branch break because the wind blew? Maybe and maybe not. This sentence is not able to give us an exact explanation of what happened.

This next example gives an exact explanation of what happened:

Because the wind blew, the branch broke.

The word *because* tells you the result: the wind blew and, as a result, the branch broke.

Activity 15G How to Use Because

In your notebook, combine these sets of sentences, using the joining word because:

1. The grass grew.
   The sun shone.   (combine . . . because)

2. The plane made an emergency landing.
   It ran out of gas.   (combine . . . because)

3. John won the dance competition.
   He practised for long hours.   (combine . . . because)

4. Gina took over a paper route.
   She wanted to buy a bicycle.   (combine . . . because)

5. Nadia enjoyed writing her poem.
   She had a good idea.   (combine . . . because)

This section talks about the word *when*. *When* is used to point out a time connection between two sentences. Look at the words in this nursery rhyme to see just how this word works:

Rockaby baby, in the tree tops,

When the wind blows, the cradle will rock,

When the bough breaks, the cradle will fall,
Down will come baby,
Cradle and all.

Explanation:
The word *when* shows the time connection between two sentences:

When something occurs, then something else happens.
The wind does not blow = the cradle does not rock.

When the wind blows = the cradle rocks.
Note that you can also write this sentence in reverse order:

The cradle rocks = when the wind blows.

Activity 15H   How to Use **When**

1. **Combine these sentences in your notebook:**
   a) **The audience sat listening.**
      The poet read his poems.   (combine . . . when)
   b) **The violinist looked startled.**
      The string broke with a sharp *twang.*   (combine . . . when)
   c) **The artist looked startled.**
      The palette fell off the stand.   (combine . . . when)

2. **Look at each picture in each set. Make up a sentence to describe the action in each picture. Write the sentences for each set in your notebook as one sentence, using** *when* **to join them.**

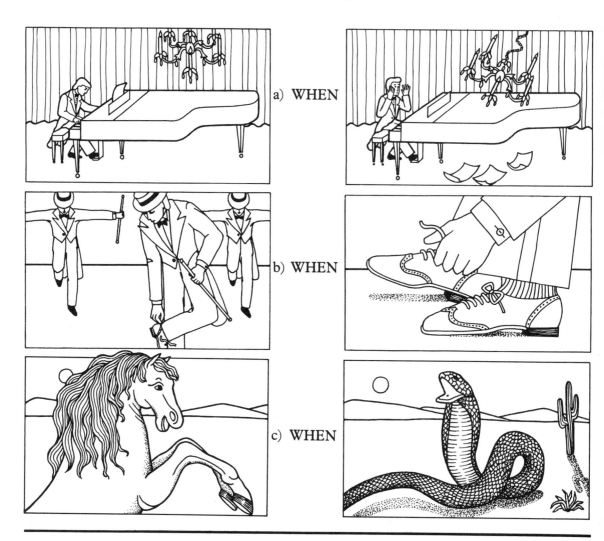

a) WHEN

b) WHEN

c) WHEN

Some other *joining words* show how sentences can be connected to indicate time connections. Look at these pictures to see how different joining words change the meaning of these two sentences:

The pitcher threw the ball.   The runner stole the base.

The pitcher threw the ball.   BEFORE The runner stole the base.

The pitcher threw the ball.   WHILE / AS   The runner stole the base.

The pitcher threw the ball.   AFTER   The runner stole the base.

A New Label
You have been using the phrase **joining words** to refer to such words as *before, while, when,* and *after.* Another phrase that describes these words is **subordinate conjunction.**

287

Activity 15I How to Use Before, While, As, *and* After

1. Combine the following sets of sentences in as many ways as possible, using the conjunctions in the box:

while/as	when	after
before	until	

2. Discuss as a whole class the difference in meaning for the sentences in each set.
   a) The explorer looked at the waterfall.
      She wrote a log in her journal.
   b) The deer looked into the forest.
      The hawk circled above.
   c) The old bear gave a signal.
      Two young cubs ambled across the clearing.

This section introduces you to one more joining word, or subordinate conjunction: *if.* Use these examples to help understand what this word means.

Which sentence describes the action in the drawing?

1. a) If the bough breaks, the cradle will fall.
   b) Since the bough is breaking, the cradle is falling.

2. a) If the storm hits, the ships will sail to the bay.
   b) Because the storm hit, the ships sailed for the bay.

3. a) If the sun shines, the crops will grow.
   b) While the sun shines, the crops grow.

The conjunction *if* tells you that something will happen in the event that something else happens. It points out the result or consequences of an action.

Activity 15ʒ How to Use **If**

1. Combine each set of sentences.
   a) I will go with you.
      You want me to go.   (combine . . . if)
   b) The team will win the championship.
      They will win one more game.   (combine . . . if)
   c) A parrot will learn to talk.
      You will train it patiently.   (combine . . . if)

2. Use your knowledge of the difference between *if* and *unless* to explain the joke in this Peanuts cartoon.

© 1959 United Feature Syndicate Inc.

Review of Subordinate Conjunctions and Labels

This section will review some of the joining words, or subordinate conjunctions, which you have studied in the last few activities. You will also learn some more labels for these words.

Review:

Read these two sentences:

| I went to the Yukon. | The snow was deep. |

As they stand here, these are two separate sentences. They are not related at all.

Watch what happens when a *joining word* is added:

> I went to the Yukon. ◁ WHEN   The snow was deep.
> (base sentence)   (base sentence)

Now the two sentences are related. The word *when* shows the connection between the ideas expressed in the two basic sentences.

Here is another example:

> I went to the Yukon. ◁ BECAUSE   The snow was deep.
> (basic sentence)   (basic sentence)

The join word *because* shows a different relationship between these sentences.

Explanation: In the first example, using *when*, the depth of the snow doesn't matter very much. "I" went there at that time. "I" probably spent my time indoors beside a swimming pool. In the second example, "I" went to the Yukon *because* there was snow there and it was deep — probably to ski.

Joining words or conjunctions can make a great deal of difference in the meaning of a sentence.

What happens to the meaning of the two basic sentences when you use *before* as the join word?

> I went to the Yukon. ◁ BEFORE   The snow was deep.
> (basic sentence)   (basic sentence)

Activity 15K   Review of Subordinate Conjunctions

Combine each set of sentences or phrases as suggested in the directions in parentheses. Remember that the symbol X means delete this word in your rewrite of the sentence.

1. Canada is underpopulated.
   Canada ~~is~~ compared to the rest of the Western World.

   (combine . . . when)

2. Prince Edward Island has the highest density of population per square kilometre in Canada.
   It has the fewest number of people.   (combine . . . although)

3. September 10, 1939, was a momentous day in Canadian history.
   Canada declared war on Germany at that time.

   (combine . . . because)

4. Canadians first paid income tax in 1917.
   Money was needed to pay for World War I.

   (combine . . . when)

5. We were officially created Canadians on January 1, 1947.
   Parliament passed the Canadian Citizenship Act.

   (combine . . . when)

6. In 1956, the Liberal Minister of Trade and Commerce, C. D. Howe, introduced closure into Parliament.
   He wanted to get the pipeline bill through the House.

   (combine . . . because)

7. The Conservative Opposition opposed the bill.
   The project was not wholly Canadian.   (combine . . . because)
   ~~It~~ was heavily financed by Americans for their own use as well.

   (combine . . . but)

8. Prince Edward Island joined Confederation in 1873.
   Canada promised to absorb a $4 million railway debt.

   (combine . . . because)
   Prince Edward Island joined.   (combine . . . if)

9. In 1957, Conservative John Diefenbaker broke the Liberal's reign in Parliament.
   The Liberals had ruled for twenty-two years from 1935.

   (combine . . . after)

10. The Gentleman Usher of the Black Rod has to knock three times.
    He is admitted to the House of Commons.   (combine . . . before)

11. He performs this ritual.
It acknowledges the people's right to freedom of speech.
(combine . . . because)

12. Charles I once jeopardized this right to free speech.
He stormed into the British House of Commons.
(combine . . . when)
H̶e̶ arrested five members. (combine . . . and)

13. The doors of the House of Commons have been kept symbolically shut.
Charles I threatened its right to free speech.
(combine . . . since)

14. British Columbia joined Confederation in 1870.
The federal government promised a transcontinental railway right to its back door. (combine . . . when)

15. The federal government was a little tardy with its promise.
The Canadian Pacific Railway did not reach British Columbia until 1885. (combine . . . because)

16. In 1775 the British expelled all the French Acadian settlers from Nova Scotia.
They had refused to swear allegiance to Britain.
(combine . . . because)
They were given exemption from British military service.
(combine . . . unless)

Labels:

The sentence structures you have been working with have names or labels. Look at these examples to identify these structures: **main clause, subordinate adverb clause, subordinate conjunction.**

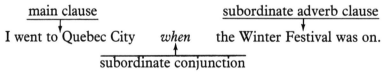

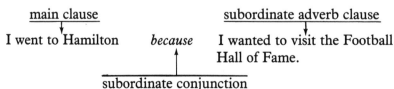

Noun Clauses

In this section, you will learn a new sentence-combining signal.

Explanation:
Look at this sentence:

> I think *that you enjoy history.*

This sentence may be represented as two base sentences, like this:

> I think *something.*
> You enjoy history.

The rewrite on this sentence is:

> I think *that* you enjoy history.

Note that the joining word, or conjunction, *that* is used to link these two ideas.
Or, try this sentence:

> I know *something.*
> Columbus discovered America.   (combine . . . that)

Rewrite: I know that Columbus discovered America.

Activity 15L   How to Use That

To fix this new signal, *something*, and the joining word *that* in your mind, try these practice sentences. Write them in your notebook as directed by the combining signals.

1. **I feel *something*.**
   Canada should defend its Arctic waters.   (combine . . . that)

2. **She suggested *something*.**
   Students should study current events.   (combine . . . that)

3. **Marvin indicated *something*.**
   Danielle had discovered a hidden city.   (combine . . . that)

   Sometimes the joining word *that* is left out of the sentence. Try these sentences, noting the signal that tells you to delete the word *that*.

4. **The Prime Minister thought *something*.**
   The Opposition would forget his words.   (combine . . . t~~h~~at)

5. In the 1960s, Prime Minister Lester B. Pearson decided *something*.
Canada should take on the role of the world's peacekeeper.
(combine . . . that)

6. Prime Minister Pearson knew *something*.
Canada should have its own flag. (combine . . . that)

Activity 15M   More Joining Words

Solve these sentence-combining problems and write the answers in your notebook.

1. The story of *something* is as interesting and inspiring as any in Canadian history.
Sir Wilfrid Laurier rose from a backwoods town to become Prime Minister. (combine . . . how)

2. Sir Wilfrid Laurier undertook to solve the problem of the separate schools in Manitoba by *something*.
We would today call "quiet diplomacy." (combine . . . what)

3. Sir Wilfrid Laurier said *something*.
"The 19th Century was the century of the United States; the 20th Century will be the century of Canada."
(combine . . . that)

4. Sir Wilfrid Laurier did not like *something*.
Britain's authority over Canada. (combine . . . X)

5. Sir Wilfrid Laurier hoped *something*.
All members of the British Empire would join together in a free and equal alliance. (combine . . . that)

These last two problems are more difficult than the others:

6. Bob Edwards wrote this quip in the *Calgary Eye Opener:*
You are only *something*.
What you are. (combine . . . X)
No one is looking. (combine . . . when)

7. The British North America Act of 1867 sets out over 147 sections.
It defines our constitutional rights. (combine . . . and)
It does not specify *something*. (combine . . . but)
The Prime Minister is to be leader of the country.
(combine . . . that)

Labels:

Here are the names for the structures you have been working with in this section.

noun clause

I know *that Canada celebrated its Centennial Year in 1967.*

noun clause

The story of *how Mr. Pearson gave Canada its flag* is filled with conflict and high emotion.

Adjective Clauses

When you combine two short sentences, you get rid of needless repetition in the sentences. For example, you could begin a report on Napoleon this way:

Napoleon Bonaparte was a great French general.
He was the son of a poor nobleman.

These two sentences seem unconnected; they stand alone. Since both sentences refer to Napoleon, you could combine them into one sentence, like this:

Napoleon Bonaparte, who was the son of a poor nobleman, was a great French general.

In this sentence, the ideas are pulled together. The word *who* shows the relationship between them.

Here are some words you can use to connect sentences:

WHICH   WHO

Example:

Napoleon married Josephine de Beauharnais.

This caret ∧
means join
the two base
sentences here.

Josephine was the widow of a French nobleman.
(combine . . . ∧who)

Rewrite:

Napoleon married Josephine de Beauharnais, *who was the widow of a French nobleman.*

Activity 15N How to Use Which *and* Who

1. Napoleon invaded Italy.
   Italy was controlled by Austria.   (combine . . ., which)

2. Napoleon drew up a code of law.
   The code of law is still used today in some countries.
   (combine . . ., which)

3. The planet Mercury was named after a Greek god.
   The god was a messenger of the gods.   (combine . . ., who)

4. Mercury has suited its name well.
   Mercury is the fastest of all planets.   (combine . . ., which . . .,)

5. Mercury is the closest planet to the sun.
   Mercury is the smallest planet of the inner planets.
   (combine . . ., which . . .,)

6. Mariner X travelled within 740 km of Mercury on March 29, 1974.
   Mariner X was the first spacecraft to reach Mercury.
   (combine . . ., which . . .,)

7. Mercury's surface is covered by a thin layer of minerals.
   Mercury's surface is like the moon's surface.
   (combine . . ., which . . .,)

8. In 1902, Madame Curie discovered and named radium.
   Madame Curie was one of the first famous women scientists.
   (combine . . ., who . . .,)

9. Madame Curie was famous throughout the world.
   Madame Curie won the Nobel Prize for physics and chemistry.
   (combine . . ., who . . .,)

INDEX